T0210073

RELAX

Jesus' Peace In the Midst of It All
Volume 1

MARDOCHEE ESTINVIL

authorHOUSE®

AuthorHouse™
1663 Liberty Drive
Bloomington, IN 47403
www.authorhouse.com
Phone: 1 (800) 839-8640

Published by AuthorHouse 07/11/2019

ISBN: 978-1-7283-1732-8 (sc)
ISBN: 978-1-7283-1731-1 (e)

Library of Congress Control Number: 2019908713

Print information available on the last page.

CONTENTS

Preface vii

Dedication xiii

Acknowledgments xv

Part One

Chapter 1   Open Space for God 1

Chapter 2   To be at peace in the midst of brokenness ... 8

Chapter 3   Forgiveness 22

Chapter 4   Christ's Presence 29

Chapter 5   Children as a Model 40

Chapter 6   Principles for Joy 46

Chapter 7   God's Will in your Personal Life 55

Chapter 8   Peace in the Darkness 63

Chapter 9   Self-control 72

Chapter 10 God is Sufficient 80

Part Two

Chapter 11 Ethical Disagreement.................................. 87

Chapter 12 A Peaceful and Successful Ministry 95

Chapter 13 Our Contribution and Support................ 115

Conclusion.. 127

Meet the Author... 129

Bibliography...135

PREFACE

A peaceful and relaxing life is possible in the midst of troubles on this earth. Many Christians and countless others are living a life of vulnerability and anxiety; a life under pressure, stress and full of worries with not much happiness. We are living at a time when numerous Christians are unnerved by the smallest issues; at a time when the "breaking news" simply breaks us down. Although at this time when fear controls the lives of many Christians seems relatively recent, this has existed for many centuries. It is important to remind ourselves that in the midst of it all we have a Savior who knows what suffering is. Knowing this brings assurance to us. Not one in our salvation but an assurance that if we keep believing and trusting in God regardless of the condition that we are facing in life, we are able to find peace in Him or to be at peace within ourselves.

Jesus said to His disciples that *"In this world you will have trouble. But take heart! I have overcome the world."* If Jesus overcame this world and we are Jesus' followers why can't we live an overcoming life? The idea of an overcome life often refers to overcoming a sinful life. However, in this one it is overcoming anxiety, vulnerability and stressful moments we face in life. It is possible to live a relaxing and peaceful life.

What do I mean by relax in this book? The word relax has sometimes been understood to mean not worrying about things or not prioritizing certain things. However, the usage of the word relax is not to minimize certain issues or to avoid thinking about them, but it is simply to maintain a sense of calm no matter the circumstances and not to allow ourselves to be controlled by an unexpected or difficult situation. As Christians we are called to live in fellowship and harmony with God through the Holy-Spirit. In contrast, what often times happens is that we allow certain issues to control us, including the media, disease, finances and countless other distractions. Since we allow these things to control us in one way or another they affect our relationship with God through His Son Jesus Christ and also how we relate to each other.

The meaning of relax in this book also has a theological projection on the understanding of God in the midst of our troubles and suffering. I am aware of the diverse interpretations of God within the Christian faith. For example, some groups of people understand the difficulties that we face as the absence of God. It is very common when someone has a problem and questions the presence of God by asking, "Where was God?" Some other groups believe that God is responsible for creating difficulties, in other words, God is the doer. Others believe that the difficulties are consequences of someone's wrongdoing, therefore God is punishing them. Another group believes that God is not creating the problems, but He allows us to face them. This list of interpretations is endless. However, all these various types of understanding of God in our suffering simply set a beautiful and enjoyable theological spectrum for us to explore and engage in.

To allow fear to control us and cause us to live a stressful life does not just exist in one or two cultures. It is a worldwide epidemic. For instance, Christians with few resources in poor countries like Haiti are controlled by thoughts of where they will find their next meal. Others who live in similarly poor countries but who have better financial access are sometimes overcome by the fear of insecurity and the fear of getting sick and not having access to medicine or urgent care. Christians in developed countries are also controlled by fear of the media, political issues, sickness, disease and so forth. Persecuted Christians who live elsewhere fear for their lives simply for being Christians or for doing the work of Christ.

Numerous churches and their preachers expound the powerful message of the second coming of Jesus. However, the problem is that while the church is preaching about the second coming of Christ, we the church should be actively fighting for social justice and social reforms. Yes, Jesus will come back again like He promised. (I strongly believe that and cannot wait for it.) However, when He returns, it will be better if He find us active rather than inactive. Clearly, this world is not ours and we should not try to change it. In contrast, we Christians are called to fulfill our calling on this earth, and this calling is based on revealing the Son as He revealed His Heavenly Father on earth. And this calling of revelation was not based only on the Son's teachings and His sermons, but it is fulfilled through His entire being. So, the term relax is not just to tell you to relax and wait for

Jesus. The purpose of embracing the term relax is to help us find peace in Jesus and to live the peaceful life that is in Him as we walk humbly and faithfully with our God on a daily basis. (It is not that we once believed, but that we keep on following and abiding in Christ).

Frequently we see happiness deriving from a material achievement in life, sometimes we think that when we have a lot of money we will be happy. Happiness does not come from what we possess. It comes from a mindset and a deep relationship with Christ. It is possible to live a relaxed and peaceful life regardless of the situation. You might be living a vulnerable life or a stressful life however it is possible to convert those sorrows and tears to living a relaxed life. *Relax* addresses some sources of the panic in our life and helps us to find a way to be at peace through those issues.

Growing up as a child, my mom and her three kids would have a devotional time every night before going to sleep. Oftentimes we would sing a song that shared the idea of "*Let mwen dormie nan bwa Jezi, Le'm reveye mwen jwen tout sa'm tap chache.*" The translation is "*When I sleep in the arms of Jesus, when I wake up I found everything that I needed.*" This song brought peace and security to me in my childhood, a message that when we trust Him or give ourselves over to Him at night that He cares for us and protects us in the middle of the night. I do believe that even if it is night or morning, wherever you might be and whomever you might be, when you abide in Jesus and keep on trusting in Him and putting yourself in His arms, He is protecting and controlling you. When we remain in Jesus and rely on His abilities in the midst of stress, worry, uncertainty, darkness, fear, disease, catastrophe and brokenness, we experience that Jesus is in control and He is more than enough. And if He is in control, if through Him we become children of God, why not relax?

DEDICATION

I dedicate this book first to my mother, who invested at least one to two hours every night on the spiritual growth of her three boys. We did this together through prayer every night, devotional and worshipping together since we were little. Although I did not understand much at that time, I now value those moments so preciously and they will always be dear to me. We still have those great moments together as long we are in the same place. Secondly, I dedicate this book to Bois Pernier a small area in Pernier, Petion-ville Haiti. This is where I started to become involved in the ministry, where I fell in love with the ministry and the place that makes me continue to love the ministry.

Thirdly, I dedicate this book to the congregation that supported me in my undergraduate school. I was blessed by the support of a congregation in the U.S. for my undergraduate studies and this has had a deep significance in my life as well. Fourthly, I dedicate 70 percent of the profit of this book for an educational fund that will be used by First Fruit Haiti and me, for establishing a training center in Haiti. One of the reasons I dedicate a significant percentage of the earnings of this book to this ministry is because very few young people that finish high school in my country have the chance to go to college. In doing so, I am giving back what I have graciously received.

ACKNOWLEDGMENTS

Without the help of many I would not be able to write this book. Many people had and continue to have a positive influence in my life. In this section, I want to acknowledge some of them.

Firstly, I want to acknowledge and thank The Creator, The Alpha and Omega, The mysteries God in Three in One. The Father, the Son and the Holy-Spirit.

Secondly, I want to acknowledge my sweet lovely beautiful wife Rachel Odmark Estinvil for supporting me in writing this book. This book has taken a lot of my time away from her. However, without a loving, kind and supportive woman like her and a woman who brings joy to my heart, I do not know how I could have written this book. Thirdly, I want to acknowledge my loving parents Miradieu and Dienata T. Estinvil, my awesome brothers Phanuel and Zacharie and my great brother in Christ, Dave Chaudry.

Fourthly, I want to acknowledge a few people outside of my family who have shaped my entire being in a positive way. Mr. Obens, my high-school coach and the first person outside of my family who helped me to trust myself, the very first person who saw and helped me develop leadership skills. Professor Amos Gabriel my friend, my professor and my mentor and who is a unique philosopher who offered me guidance. Mrs. Sophia Botello, my English professor and the person who gave me a lot of free assistance and help with the content of this book at the writing center at Baptist University of the Americas.

The list could go on and on, but I want to thank each and every person who has helped me throughout the process of writing this book and those who have influenced my life in a positive way. Special thanks to the editor Lynne Feldman and thanks to the publishing company.

PART ONE

ON A PERSONAL LEVEL

CHAPTER ONE

OPEN SPACE FOR GOD

It is not just 2016 and 2017 that had gone upside down with political issues, natural disasters and countless other terrible things that have shaken our being. The way the 21st century has begun has shaken our very existence. One of the major fears in 1999 was whether or not computers would work on the first day of the 21st century. A year and nine months later, with broken hearts we observed the destruction of the World Trade Center. Following this devastation, a declaration of war changed our world. Other places in the world faced famine, illiteracy and political instability.

As years pass new issues start emerging, including economic crises across the world, tsunamis in several countries and the tragic and unforgettable earthquake that shook Port-Au-Prince Haiti, leaving many without a home, many losing a loved one, either a family member or a close friend and many without the resources to start over. This earthquake took over 200,000 lives.

Worldwide, violent people with guns ravage communities causing many innocent people to die. November 5th, 2017 is an example of this, when one out of control person entered a Texas church and killed more than 20 people. On October 1, 2017 a person killed many people at a concert in Las Vegas. In some other places guns have been used by many to pressure someone either to steal or to kidnap and ask for ransom.

Such catastrophes swirl around us in public places, each person carrying his or her own issues that affect them at a personal or at a family level. Facing these crises clearly demonstrates that being people of God does not prevent us nor does it mean that we can escape the ravages of misfortune. We are challenged to face these events and it is of great importance how we face these challenges. Life is often shaky, problems come in succession and those problems are real. Despite this reality, it should not prevent us from living peacefully.

One night during my honeymoon in St. Petersburg we were in the middle of a sweet and lovely snuggle. After a wonderful day visiting this beautiful city's downtown, my lovely wife Rachel and I were thinking of some challenges that we were about to face after the honeymoon. These included a driving adventure from Minnesota to San Antonio when Rachel would move all her belongings, the mission trip to Haiti that we were going to lead in around 20 days and finding jobs soon after we returned from Haiti. Finding the job after the mission trip to Haiti was one of the biggest stresses. The problem was that Rachel had applied for several jobs two months before the wedding and had not yet received any responses. As we continued to snuggle, I lay quietly with her head on my skinny arms but I did not know what to say. After a little while I said: *"Open space."* Again, I said *"Open space."* But it was on the third time that I actually understood it to mean *"Open space for God."*

These words were not simply for my lovely wife Rachel, but they were also for me. The phrase "open space" was not for us to open space from snuggling, it was simply to open space for God for those challenges we would face. It is a human sense and our instinct to rule and to be fully in control of everything that is happening around us. This is very good and very smart, yet it is very important to remind ourselves that sometimes we cannot be fully in control. The great thing is that when we face these anomalies, our job as Christians is simply to open space for God. Our job is not to be stressed about these matters nor should we allow these things to prevent us from being at peace. It is simply a moment in life where we apply humility by opening space for God.

Open space for God is an act of faith. To open space is simply to surrender the problem to God. It does not mean that we are ignorant of the issue. However, we accept the reality, we embrace it and even more importantly we know that Christ knows, and He empathizes with us in our weakness. The greatness, goodness and power of our God are unbelievable and unexplainable. Even more, one thing that shakes me the most is to know that His Son Jesus knows what suffering is. The apostle Paul said: *"For we do not have a high priest who is unable to empathize with our weaknesses, but we have one who has been tempted in every way, just as we are—yet he did not sin. Let us then approach God's throne of grace with confidence, so that we may receive mercy and find grace to help us in our time of need"* (Hebrews 4:15-16 NIV). To know that Jesus Christ understands what weakness is sets us in a place to trust Him more and to open space. Not only this, in the verse we find the invitation to go to Him just as we are as we approach Him with confidence.

Numerous times when we think or want to control issues on our own, we end up lost and confused. This can even lead to depression. There are several things that can lead to depression, but one of the ways people become depressed is from holding onto stress or trying to handle a difficulty on their own. We all face challenges, but we are not called to face them alone. Let Christ be in control of it all, as we open space for the Holy-Spirit to move in us.

I had the chance to interview a pastor who has been involved in ministry for several years. In his ministry he has ministered in several churches in the U.S and in Mexico. He has ministered a number of people who struggled with depression and he himself had gone through a very difficult time in his life.

For him, suffering and difficulties are inevitable. They are things that Christians and non-Christians face. However, the way a person faces those difficult moments is very important because it can either bring that person closer to God or it can bring doubt in his or her faithful life. It can even make a person stop believing in the existence of God. For Him, it all depends on how we understand certain things, and this will either bring us closer to God or moves us away from God. If we believe that God is unjust because He lets bad things happen, we are moving away from God rather than bringing Him close to us. (The pastor's point is not that we should not be honest with God but being honest is not an opportunity to blame God.) The pastor suggested that during such difficulties, it is very important to understand that people hurt people, and Christ knows and understands what weaknesses are. It is to understand that we are limited in our own selves and we cannot handle a lot. Not only does the pastor give suggestions to those who are facing such a difficult time, but even more he believes that Christians and the church have an obligation to help those who are facing depression.[1] When we know an individual is struggling, it is important to include it as part of our duty to support that person however we can.

In the gospels we read about numerous healings and miracles of Jesus. In many of these healings and miracles, there was always a need or a problem that needed a solution and there was also space for Christ. As Christians we will surely encounter a lot of difficulties in life and this is normal, we are not escapers of trouble. However, we can relax and live peacefully when we open space for God. When we do so, we are simply surrendering ourselves to Him. Through our surrendering, we find peace and tranquility. Paul in his letter to the Philippians said*: "Do not be anxious about anything, but in every situation, by prayer and petition, with thanksgiving, present your requests to God. And the peace of God, which transcends all understanding, will guard your hearts and your minds in Christ Jesus"* (Philippians 4:6-7 NIV). One interesting thing about this letter is that when Paul wrote this letter he was in prison.

We surrender ourselves to God through prayer. Prayer is the key way to communicate with God. However, frequently in our prayers we act like we are leaving a voice mail to God or we are asking God to work according to our will.

---

[1] Pastor X, *Personal Interview by Mardochee Estinvil*, San Antonio: November 2017.

It is very important in our prayer through Christ to speak and to listen. Remember, it is not all about our own will, but that God's will is even more important. When we open space for God, we understand Him better and we build a stronger relationship with Him. To open space primarily requires trust, to open space is an act of faith. It is not an act of laziness or an act of ignorance.

When my wife and I were thinking about the challenges of driving from Minnesota to Texas, the mission trip to Haiti and finding a job, we opened space for God and as we did so we could simply see God's glory manifesting. The driving experience came out well, the mission trip to Haiti was wonderful and we found the job at the exalted moment that we needed it. A few months afterwards, I was looking back at this experience while I was on a walk. I reminded myself that I'm not alone on this journey of life. My responsibility is to do my very best, but it is also to open space for God in each and every detail. Numerous times we panic and feel stress and we act like orphans. What we need to do is constantly remind ourselves that we are not alone on this life journey, and that Christ is with us through the Holy Spirit. It is vital for a Christian to open space for God and to let Christ be in control.

King David, during a very difficult moment in his life, wrote a powerful Psalm that is well-known in many languages around the world. Psalm 23, "The Lord is my Shepherd." In this phrase there are two key words. The first is *Lord*, the everlasting God, the glorious One, the Holy and Wise One, the One that is self-sufficient and worthy of adoring. The second key word is *Shepherd*. This means that the Lord is not just everlasting, but He is also compassionate. The Lord is not just self-sufficient, but He is also self-sacrificing for His people.[2] As the Lord is such a God, David is able to find rest, refreshment and joy in the Lord's presence. David continues and says how he finds guidance, how the Lord walks and protects him in the difficulties.

Psalm 23 has impacted countless people's lives in different ways. Helping people with troubles find peace and helping broken people find comfort. This psalm is impactful, and it impacts differently depending on the reader and the reader's needs. I cannot think of a better way to finish this chapter than through the reading of this Psalm.

Let's pray:

"1 The LORD IS MY SHEPHERD, I LACK NOTHING.
2 He makes me lie down in green pastures,
he leads me beside quiet waters,
3 he refreshes my soul. He guides me along
the right paths for his name's sake.
4 Even though I walk through the darkest valley, I will fear
no evil, for you are with me your rod and your staff, they
comfort me. 5 You prepare a table before me in the presence of
my enemies. You anoint my head with oil; my cup overflows.
6 Surely your goodness and love will
follow me all the days of my life,
and I will dwell in the house of the LORD
forever" (Psalm 23 NIV).

---

[2] James Hastings, ed., *The Great Texts of the Bible, Vol. 3* (Grand Rapids: Wm. B. Eerdmans, 1958).

Chapter Two

To be at peace in the midst of brokenness

Moments of brokenness are for sure the period of life that everyone would love to skip. We definitely do not like moments in life when we are broken. Moments when we do not know what to do, nor can we understand or think clearly. It is something that each and every one of us experiences in a different way. Although we each can experience it differently and do not like those moments in life, brokenness is something that we face or can face several times in life. As it is something that we face in our Christian life's journey, it is important to go through it in a peaceful, relaxing and trusting way. It is not a moment to doubt faith or reproach God, rather it is a unique moment to experience God differently. It is these experiments that will bring us closer to Him.

Often when we face broken moments in life, we misuse what it means to be open to God. It is important in our relationship with God to be open and honest with Him. However, being open to God does not mean blaming God or seeing Him as the one who has made a mistake.

That does not mean that I'm not pragmatic about this matter, in fact if there is one person that does not like those moments in life know that I am the one. As we encounter these moments of brokenness in our walk with Christ, it is important to get it right and to be at peace in the midst of it all. Often our reactions to broken moments are similar to those of the Israelites when they found themselves in the wilderness when things were not going well. They started to reproach Moses, forgetting where God had taken them and forgetting what God had already accomplished for them.

How we interpret these broken moments

Brokenness is a phase or a moment that has different ways of being understood by various Christians. For some, being broken is viewed as a moment of absence from God. This group believes that the cause of a broken moment in life is based on a mistake that you once committed, and due to this failure it affects your personal relationship with God. In short, for this group to face a broken moment in life as a Christian is the result of a wrong doing. An example of this ideology is found in the powerful story of Job in the Bible, when Job's friends informed him that he must have had done something bad in the eyes of God. For God to allow him to face such difficult moments in his life, it meant that Job did something wrong. For many, a broken moment in life is the result of a sinful act.

Another stream in this spectrum of understanding defines brokenness as God's way of testing us. This stream not only sees God allowing or permitting these things to happen, but also sees God being responsible for doing these things. Those that disagree with this stream of understanding hold the conviction that God will never test us because He knows everything, and that God does not want any bad things to happen to His children.

Others see brokenness as a process in which God is teaching us and preparing us for a higher level or a new chapter in our life's journey. Some great examples of this ideology are provided when Moses fled Egypt when the Pharaoh accused him of killing an Egyptian. In Moses' broken moments, God placed him as the leader He would use to deliver the Israelites away from the Egyptian. Moses the man before the brokenness and Moses the man who was talking to God after being broken are two different men, but yet the same person. Another example is the moment when David's family did not value him, the moment when he had no value in the eyes of his family. Yet at this time God was preparing him to become the King of the Israelites.

In these various interpretations of brokenness, my standpoint is that none of these streams is fully wrong or fully right. However, my main interest in this chapter is not in any of these streams of thought, but more in our walks with Christ in the midst of the broken moments in life. I am more interested that we find a balance of being at peace and relaxed in the midst of it all, to enjoy the goodness of God during the hardships. I am not so concerned with the deliverance during the broken moments in life, but to let those moments be a unique and unforgettable moment between God and us. One of the things that appears frequently is that in our broken moments the type of message we want to hear is one of deliverance. A message of God will deliver you and God will make miracles happen. Certainly,

I am not against the message of miracles. In fact, I believe in this message, but the problem is that too frequently we focus so much on deliverance from the hardship and we miss out on the message that God wants to fulfill at that specific moment. Another problem appears when we focus too much on miracles, we allow this obsession with miracles to control us, and this often causes us to miss a meaningful relationship with God. In other words, we end up not enjoying the relationship that we could have had with God in the midst of those broken moments.

When will the broken moments end:

I for sure do not know if the broken moments you have faced or will face are just for a limited time in your life or if it is something that you will endure for a lifetime. In the Bible we see people who faced brokenness for a moment in their life on earth while others encountered brokenness until their death. One example of this is found in the parable of the rich man and Lazarus. I am citing this parable to demonstrate the hardship that Lazarus endured until he died. In the gospel of Luke, we read this story and the text tells us that Lazarus was a beggar and he died begging in front of the rich man's house. (Luke 16:19-31). For Lazarus, being broken was not just a season in his life, but it was what he faced until the day he died. I am not telling you that the moments of brokenness you have been faced with will end soon or that the broken moments you might face will be for a short period of time. I wish I knew what was in store for you so that I could tell you. However, what I am advocating

11

is that you must remain in and abide in Christ; along the way you are not alone and through it all Christ is with you.

The outcome of a research

Brokenness is a very difficult moment that we go through and there are many things that can create these moments. For instance, the death of a loved one, a critical diagnosis and illness of a loved one and countless other heartbreaks can trigger a broken moment for someone. The impact of that broken moment in the life of a person can create depression, a universal response. Both Christians and non-Christians alike face depression in life.

I conducted research on depression as I realized how common the issue was among many people. I sat down with several people who suffer from depression and with those who had overcome depression. The idea was to first listen and try to understand what they were going through and how they could or already have overcome it.

It is important to first acknowledge that there are mainly two types of depression. There is one that is identified as genetically transmitted—when someone suffers from depression because their parents themselves had the same disease. The second one and the one that I am focusing on is the depression that develops because of crises surfacing around a person. For example: someone that is going through a big family crisis can suffer depression. This type of depression is created by the impact of a broken moment in someone's life. It is not the broken moment in itself that automatically created depression. However, it is the way that this broken moment controlled the person which created depression. In other words, it is how the person manages the difficulties that will make the difference.

There are many things that cause depression, but one of the most common factors is based on the circumstances of life. Family problems, concern about the future and, one that was difficult for me to understand, low self-esteem. (Low self-esteem brings someone to depression through self-comparing to another person. This can bring the person to think that he or she is inferior to another person.) Depression primarily manifests itself in two ways emotionally. The first is upside down (see Figure 1). The second one is mostly a very deep shadow that someone is in (see Figure 2).

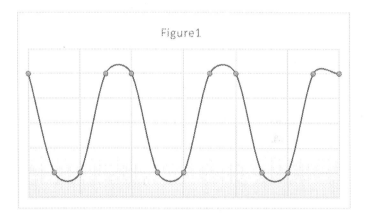

Figure 1

Figure 1 is what I identify as the upside-down way. In this one, the up represents a person feeling happy or content and the down represents when the person is depressed. However, up does not mean the problem is completely gone from the person's life.

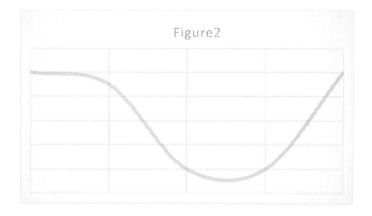

Figure 2

Figure 2 is the *shadow* in a person's life. It does not go up. It simply stays down and might eventually come up, depending on the person or the assistance and support that this person receives. A good way to illustrate this figure is like a person who is going along a long road that is very dark and this person sees only darkness.

Accepting and Embracing

Unfortunately, we cannot escape the reality of life which involves both happy and broken moments. We cannot escape the reality of life neither can we skip the sad moments in life. However, we can go through these broken moments in a very peaceful and relaxing way. In the research I conducted on depression, one of the things that everyone shared who had been healed and was free from depression was that they all accepted and embraced their reality. This was the very first step for them. It is important to embrace and accept the broken moments, not questioning why or asking God, where is He?

One of the most powerful testimonies of someone who healed was a man who I had talked to during my research. The man had struggled with depression for around 28 years of his life. It had started at a very young age, when he was experiencing a lot of difficulties and struggles. He even attempted suicide twice. After 25 years, he embraced his issues, accepted them and said to the Lord "that I will accept and embrace these issues and I know these issues will simply be for my good." After saying this, his healing started. In less than three years after saying that and involving himself in helping others, he overcame the depression and was healed from it. That does not mean that he never again faced any troubling issues in his life after that, nor does it suggest that he never again became sad, but he was able to be at peace in the broken moments that he would later face. He was able to overcome depression. Embracing and accepting broken moments as a Christian is to believe that these things will help me grow in Christ. It is to believe that I'm not caring or handling these problems alone or with my own strength, but that the Holy Spirit is here with me.

There is a very well-known verse from the Apostle Paul in the book of Romans. It said *And we know that all things work together for good to them that love God, to them who are the called according to his purpose"* (Romans 8:28 KJV). This verse does not mean that the empty moments, broken moments, overwhelming and stressful moments that we face in life are good. However, for those who love God, these bad moments beneficially serve us. Paul the Apostle, who himself said *"that all things work together for good to them that love God"* was one that understood what suffering was and faced many difficult moments in his life. *"We know"* meaning we are certain and confident that even in the most difficult moments in life there is a fulfillment of great things for those who love God. *"Good"* meaning in our advantage, in our interest, in our benefit. However, this benefit can be misunderstood. The meaning of good sometimes and many times supersedes our human comprehension. An example is; one of the most shameful deaths in the history of humanity—the crucifixion of Jesus Christ. We learned that death in itself is not good or fun. However, this crucifixion worked for the greater good of humanity. We embrace, accept, face the difficulties and through these actions we find peace. We find peace not in our own capacity, but in Christ.

Living by the Holy Spirit

Life is a paradox. It is filled with good moments that we love and enjoy. Life also has many difficult moments that make us struggle and even cry sometimes. Life teaches us that we are blessed, but it also teaches us that we do not earn anything. Life demonstrates that we are creatures that are blessed to enjoy things. (The meaning of enjoying is not a pass to get drunk or go crazy with drugs). However, we are to be grateful and mindful of every single thing. As lovely as life can be, it can also become sad and stressful. No matter how difficult life can be, giving up should never be an option. We can always be at peace.

Those who abide in Christ experience both good and bad moments in their life's journey. People who abide in and remain in Christ do so by building a foundation based on a relationship rather than on circumstances. In other words, the relationship with Christ defines those who remain in Him. They are not defined by the bad circumstances they faced in life. Due to this great relationship with God through Christ, we are able to live at peace even in the midst of brokenness. This is the relationship we Christians live in and by the Holy Spirit.

The Holy Spirit is one of God's greatest gifts to those who believe and follow Him. The Holy Spirit had a deeper meaning for the early disciples than it does for many Christians today. One of the reasons for this difference is because these disciples had given up all their life to follow Jesus and knowing that their master would be gone was deeply sad for them. The ultimate comfort and trust of the early disciples were found in Jesus and hearing Jesus tell them that He will no longer physically be with them caused them to feel desperate. Nevertheless, Jesus in His love for His early disciples did not leave them alone; He gave the disciples and to all those who believed in Him the Holy Spirit. In other words, Jesus is no longer physically present with us. However, Jesus gave us the Holy Spirit in which we can still experience the power and comfort of Christ through this spirit.

There are many, if not countless, roles that the Holy Spirit plays, including a comforter, a guide, a helper, a teacher, the one who unifies us with God, the one who helps us to transform in the likeness of Christ and so on. Despite all these roles that the Holy Spirit plays, the role of comforter is the role that will be addressed in this section.

It is important to acknowledge that similar to salvation, we do not earn the Holy Spirit. Some action is needed to receive and live in and by the Holy Spirit. In other words, to live in and by the Holy Spirit, some personal action is needed, a decision is required to be made and a different style of life is essential. Two great examples of personal needs are obedience and self-surrendering. Part of living by the Holy Spirit is to acknowledge that my will is ungodly. The Holy Spirit helps us to find the Christ-like option or to help us find the Christ-like way of responding, but the Holy Spirit does not always make decisions for us. Therefore, self-obedience is necessary to allow the Holy Spirit to work. I will not go into more detail, but my point in this paragraph is that in order to live by the Holy Spirit, there is the need of taking personal responsibility.

When we live by the Holy Spirit, the Spirit helps us to understand the *purpose* of our life and how to find *peace* in no other place than in Christ. *Purpose*: part of our purpose is not living for our own self or to be attached too much with the materialistic world. Our purpose in life is to focus on living for God alone. To focus on doing what is best for the Kingdom of God. *Peace in Christ*: we are not strong or bold enough to handle the reality of life in our own capacity. And thanks to God we find strength in abiding and remaining in Christ. The difficulties of life do not drive us, but our spirituality and faith thrive in those bad circumstances. We do not focus on the self, but in Christ alone. We go through these broken moments not in our own strength, but into the ultimate reliability and dependency on God.

Paul said, *"[T]hat all things work together for good to them that love God"* and these were not simply words for him, but things that filled his life. He faced a lot of difficulties in his life. He was persecuted and even went to prison because he preached the Gospel. One of the most powerful books of joy in the New Testament is the book of Philippians. Paul is the author of this book; he wrote this book while he was in prison and this book was a letter from Paul to the church in Philippi.

Prison is not the best place to be in life and it is not a place where you find inspiration to write about joy. As a prisoner you might write about joy if you are writing about a great experience in the past or a fun experience that will come once you are out of prison. For the Apostle Paul, his contentment and joy did not depend on where he was or what he was facing or on his own personal capacity, but it did depend on him being in Christ. It all depended on Paul living by the Holy Spirit. In other words, the apostle did not find joy and comfort in the place where he was, but he found his comfort in the Holy Spirit.

Jesus in His teachings never told His disciples that life would be easy for them in this world. In fact, Jesus told His disciples that people would hate them, and people would persecute them. This is not just for the early disciples, but also for Christians today. Our life journey in this world is not easy and will not be easy. We each face different forms of difficulties in life and it is normal, but thanks to our Heavenly Father and His son Jesus for providing the Holy Spirit, for when we live by the Holy Spirit we are at peace in a broken world and we find comfort even in the calamities.

Our Contribution

Before I conducted research on depression, I saw things on a personal level. What this means is that it was all about a personal responsibility to be at peace in difficult moments. After I finished researching depression I came to the understanding that yes there is a personal level that is strongly needed, but there is also the need of a spiritual and communal contribution to support and help those people that are going through a difficult moment. This part is fully developed in the chapter entitled, "Our Contribution and Support."

Conclusion

There was a man named Joseph Scriven. He was born in Ireland in 1819. In 1845 one day before his wedding in Ireland, his fiancée was found drowned in a river. Sadly, after the tragedy the young man decided to move to Canada where he started a new life.[3] He dedicated his time to helping and serving others with no charge. He then became engaged for a second time and a week or two before the wedding his fiancée died from a disease. Sometime after, Joseph received a letter from his mother that she was critically ill.

In response to his mother's letter, Joseph Scriven wrote her a letter of comfort that was published a few years later as the hymn, "What a friend we have in Jesus."[4] In this hymn, we see the presence of sorrow and pain, but even more importantly we see that there is a friend that knows what weakness is and that we can also bring the problems to Jesus in prayer.

---

[3] Robert J. Morgan, *Then Sings My Soul* (Nashville: Thomas Nelson Publisher, 2003), 131.

[4] "The Story Behind the Hymn: 'What a Friend We Have in Jesus,'" Stuarts Draft Retirement Community (blog). October 30, 2013. Accessed January 03, 2018. http://www.sdretire.com

Even through all the broken moments and sad experiences that Joseph Scriven experienced in his life, he could still find comfort in a friendship with Christ. We all face difficulties in life, but like Joseph Scriven once said, "We should never be discouraged. Take it to the Lord in prayer."[5] We embrace and accept the reality, but we do not carry it in our own strength. We focus on our relationship with the God of the Universe through the Holy Spirit.

---

[5] "What a Friend we have in Jesus," Hymn alnet RSS. Accessed January 3, 2018. https://www.hymnal.net/en/home

CHAPTER THREE

FORGIVENESS

"It is nearly impossible to be at peace, when you are holding bitterness and anger inside of you."

When it comes to my own personal list of some disciplines of Jesus, a discipline that is not only hard to practice but one that I do not like is forgiveness. However, the instructions of Jesus are not given to us simply because He wants us to follow them. Even more, these instructions are given to us primarily because they are the best for our life.

To forgive someone is not always logical, but it does not have to be logical. Forgiveness is not about what one person did to you or to someone else and it is not about whether the person deserves to be forgiven. Forgiveness is not based on how hurtful the act was nor is it based on whether the person is conscious of his or her own wrongdoing. Forgiveness is all about you, the victim. Forgiveness is about your way of responding to that wrongdoing. Forgiveness does not focus on the other, but simply focuses on you. It is very important to understand that forgiveness only depends on you, without any responsibility placed on the other person.

There are at least four major things that forgiveness does. First, it allows you to let the bitterness and anger go. It sets you free from holding that bitterness and anger inside. The second thing that forgiveness does is that it helps those that practice it understand and reflect God better. Third, it sets the stage for reconciliation. Finally, forgiveness demonstrates that compassion, love and grace are greater than revenge and a response of anger.

Letting the Bitterness and Anger Go

To not forgive is to hold bitterness and anger inside, either about something that someone once did or something that one person might have done to his or her own self. To forgive first requires letting go of the bitterness and anger, although, it is not easy to let the hurtful and painful memory go.

There is a lady who lost her mom at a very young age. Ever since she lost her mom she has been living with her grandmother. Even though her father knows of her existence, not even for one day has she ever felt the presence of her dad, nor has her dad ever tried to reach her. Not even for one day of her life has her father supported her with any financial assistance. Deep inside of this young girl, there is that sad and hurtful memory of her dad. Every time I have had the chance to hear her talking and by accident she mentions her personal life, she immediately starts crying and says that there is no possible way for her to forgive her father. For sure, her father does not deserve to be forgiven, but the saddest thing is the impact of holding that bitterness and anger inside of her. This has significantly affected her life.

To forgive is not an act that approves the wrongdoing as right. To forgive is a beneficial act to the one who practices it. It is to let the bitterness and anger go. When someone practices forgiveness, he or she lets the bad memories go. There is absolutely no positivity in holding bitterness and anger inside. Forgiveness brings freedom.

Corrie Ten Boom is a great woman of influence. She had experienced numerous struggles during World War II when her family hid Jews from the Nazi's inhumanity. After the war, she opened her home in Holland for the victims of that brutality. One of the things she said about the people that were able to return to the outside world and rebuild their lives was that they were able to forgive their former enemies, regardless of the physical and emotional scars. Those who continued to hold the bitterness were not able to move forward.[6] Forgiveness frees the one who practices it.

Understands and Reflects God Better

Forgiveness helps those that practice it understand that humankind is imperfect. Not only is humankind imperfect but human beings can also be foolish, arrogant and prejudiced. By recognizing this, one can understand how painful and hurtful it is to God when we sin. We all in some measure act and react wrongly, and we need forgiveness. Not only do we need it, but we also need to practice forgiveness to others. It is stated in the Lord's Prayer, *"And forgive us our*

---

[6] Corrie Ten Boom, *Clippings from my notebook: writings and sayings collected* (Minneapolis: World Wide Publications, 1984), 93-94.

debts, as we also have forgiven our debtors." (Matthew 6:9-13 NIV). Forgive us in the same way we forgive those who do us wrong.

The Lord's Prayer is not the prayer of Paul or Peter; it was the prayer that Jesus taught His disciples after they had asked Him to teach them how to pray. Right inside of this prayer, we find the inclusion of forgiveness. And forgiveness is not simply being asked from us to God but set in a form where we ask God to forgive us in the same way we forgive others. In other words, the need is not simply us needing to be forgiven, but also, we need to forgive others. For in the way we forgive others, it is in that same way and level you will be forgiving. We cannot fully understand God, but we can understand a little bit more of Him every time we forgive someone who did us wrong.

An amazing thing about being a Christian is that the person is not simply a believer, but the person is also one that is called to reflect Christ throughout his or her life. A Christian duty is not simply to talk about God's love to others, but it is also to demonstrate that love of God to others. We reflect God's mercy when we forgive.

Forgiveness Sets the Place for Reconciliation

It is important to acknowledge that simply forgiving someone will not bring reconciliation. For someone to reconcile requires the involvement of the other person's consciousness and action for it to happen. However, when we do our part, which is to forgive, we set space for reconciliation. After the failure of humankind, God made His redemptive plan for all human beings through the death of His son Jesus Christ on the Cross. God has opened space to rebuild the relationship between Him and us through Jesus. However, in order for this reconciliation to take place in someone's life, there is the need of that person's consciousness to accept that we *"all have sinned, and come short of the glory of God"* (Romans 3:23 KJV). Not only the conscious act is needed, but there is also the action of believing which will lead to repentance and many other things. When we forgive, we open space and give space for reconciliation.

God does not simply want His believers to get their relationship right with Him, but God also wants His children to get their relationship right with all other people. Therefore, it is very important to set space for reconciliation and it will not happen unless we truly learn to forgive and understand the meaning of forgiveness. Forgiveness does not simply bring peace within oneself, but it also brings peace and reconciliation to our relationships with others.

Compassion, Love and Grace are Greater than Revenge and a Response of Anger

The story of Joseph is a very popular one that many people know well. It is the story of a young man who was his father's favorite. Joseph's brothers were so jealous of him that they wanted to kill him, but after putting him into a dry well they sold him into slavery. His brothers were unable to tell their father what they had done to his favorite son. They decided to put the blood of an animal on Joseph's clothes and then brought the clothes to their father and told him that Joseph had died. After this, Joseph was no longer treated as their father's favorite son, but was working and living like a slave. Having the blessing of the Lord on him, this young man was promoted by his master. Joseph was given authority over every single thing the master had in his house except over the master's wife. Just as bad things can happen to anyone bad things can happen to people of God. This happened to Joseph as he was sent to prison when the master's wife falsely accused him. God selected Joseph to become the prime minister of Egypt. He was next in line to the King. When famine threatened many people, they and Joseph's brothers came looking for food in Egypt (Genesis 37-41).

When Joseph's brothers arrived in Egypt to buy food, they saw their brother Joseph. Joseph as prime minister could easily get his revenge or react in anger towards his brothers. However, Joseph chose the compassionate way and opened opportunities in Egypt for all of his brothers. He helped his brothers to see the positive side of their wrongdoing. Forgiveness promotes compassion, love and grace, forgiveness demonstrates that these things are greater than revenge. Joseph could easily have taken revenge, but the question is what good would come out of it? When we forgive, we find peace in two ways: peace in our mind and we open space for reconciliation.

There are freedom and peace in forgiving. Forgiveness is a conscious act and it can be very difficult to forgive someone. I have provided a short exercise for forgiveness followed by a prayer.

A Short Exercise for Forgiveness

    a.   Describe the issue?
    b.   Describe the pain it created?
    c.   The reason not to forgive?
    d.   Now make the decision to forgive the act.
    e.   Why should I forgive?

Let's Pray

Heavenly Father,
it is so very hard to forgive sometimes
it is not that logic in our human comprehension.
However, when I think of how much I have been forgiven
through your son Jesus Christ I understand my duty to forgive.
Please give me the strength and the courage to forgive.
In the name of your son, I pray. Amen.

CHAPTER FOUR

CHRIST'S PRESENCE

The fall of 2016 was a very difficult time for me. The first thing that shocked me was the natural disaster that struck Haiti in September. This disaster destroyed a lot of things, mostly in the south of this beautiful country. Throughout this tragedy I was doing my best to keep myself in a happy mood. However, sometime around the end of November while I was checking my social media, I saw a friend's post that was giving courage to another friend of mine. As soon as I saw this post, I contacted my friend and tried to find out what happened. Sadly, I heard the news that her older sister had been killed. A young woman who had her entire life before her got shot several times and died, leaving behind a son, her family and her friends devastated by this tragedy.

It was during this very sad period of my life that I began to realize that it was not only I who was going through a difficult moment, but numerous others were also going through difficult moments because of politics or other complicated matters. In places like Haiti, the difficult moment was political instability as the country tried to recover from the natural disaster and tried to deal with other reasons. In this period, I was looking for understanding: "Why is Haiti so unlucky?" "Why does someone choose to take someone's life away and leave their loved ones in sadness?" "Did this person not have a better option?" At the same time, others were raising different questions. Questions about politics in general, how certain people get elected. People in Haiti raised the following question: "Really! After this natural disaster we as a nation still cannot come to a political agreement?"

At that same time, I did not find what I was looking for but more importantly I found what I needed. What I needed was comfort, that even with all this sadness and uncertainty I could be at peace. The passage in which I found my comfort, which was also my Christmas passage, is found in John 20: 19-29.

On the evening of that first day of the week, when the disciples were together, with the doors locked for fear of the Jewish leaders, Jesus came and stood among them and said, "Peace be with you." After he said this, he showed them his hands and side. The disciples were overjoyed when they saw the Lord. Again Jesus said, "Peace be with you! As the Father has sent me, I am sending you." And with that he breathed on them and said, "Receive the Holy Spirit. If you forgive anyone's sins, their sins are forgiven; if you do not forgive them, they are not forgiven." Now Thomas (also known as Didymus[a]), one of the Twelve, was not with the disciples when Jesus came. So the other disciples told him, "We have seen the Lord!" But he said to them, "Unless I see the nail marks in his hands and put my finger where the nails were, and put my hand into his side, I will not believe." A week later his disciples were in the house again, and Thomas was with them. Though the doors were locked, Jesus came and stood among them and said, "Peace be with you!" Then he said to Thomas, "Put your finger here; see my hands. Reach out your hand and put it into my side. Stop doubting and believe." Thomas said to him, "My Lord and my God!" Then Jesus told him, "Because you have seen me, you have believed; blessed are those who have not seen and yet have believed."

This portion of scripture has been traditionally referred to on or used for Easter Sunday to celebrate the resurrection of Jesus. Even though this biblical text describes the appearance of Jesus to his disciples on the third day after His crucifixion, the message that is contained within this portion can be shared at different times throughout the year.

In the text we read of the disciples being afraid, hiding inside of a room and locking the door. The reason why they were inside of the locked room was because of the death of Jesus. Although Jesus had died and the disciples knew about His resurrection, they were still overcome by fear. Now, it is quite easy to point out the disciples' unbelief or fear, but like the disciples we too are overcome by fear and doubt. Fear is an emotion that humankind has been facing throughout history, and fear has had great control over us as human beings. The cause of these fears has been different over time and has also been expressed in different forms depending on the location. As an example, after the attack on the World Trade Center, most people in the U.S were driven with the fear of terrorist attacks, while some people in underdeveloped countries were worried about political instability or hunger. Therefore, the fear in each shift has been different and has been expressed in different ways.

Unlike the disciples, today we do not share the fear of Jesus' death, but we do have fear of the media, of becoming sick and of being persecuted. Our fear does not hold us in a small room rather fear holds us in our own circle. The impact of fear for both the disciples and for us today is the same, keeping us in our small self-contained circles, which prevents the sharing of great news.

The disciples saw many of Jesus' great miracles and heard many of his teachings and yet that did not prevent them from being controlled by fear. This is no different from us because we know that Jesus died for our sins. He overcame death. We have read of His teachings and the Holy Spirit has been made available to us. Even with all of these truths, we continue to be controlled by fear or by our bad circumstances in life. This brings to attention that simply knowing is not enough to live free of fear. To know is not enough to prevent anyone from being overcome or controlled by fear and doubts.

In the scriptural text we read that in the midst of the disciples' fear, Jesus appeared to them and said, *"Peace be with you"* (John 20:19 NIV). He showed them proof and the text tell us that the disciples' sadness turned to joy. What the disciples experienced was peace from Jesus through His presence among them. It has been stated that the phrase "Peace be with you" was a traditional greeting at that time. Although it was a traditional greeting, this phrase had a new and deeper meaning for the disciples.[7]

---

[7] Morgan, G. Campbell, *The Gospel According to John* (London and Edinburgh: Fleming H. Revell Company, 1933), 317.

"*Peace be with you*" sounded different and more powerful than it had ever sounded for them before. The word *peace* is translated in Greek as *eirene*[8] and one of the meanings of this word is tranquility. In the midst of their fear, Jesus brought tranquility, safety and relaxation into their hearts.

What is interesting is the power that changed the disciples' sadness to joy. And this did not come from the words "*Peace be with you,*" but from the One who spoke these words. The tension that the disciples found themselves in required a powerful source; if these words were coming from someone else it would not have had such a powerful impact. Within my own understanding of this portion, I believe that the phrase "*Peace be with you*" is simply a description of Jesus' presence in the midst of His disciples. In other words, it was Jesus' presence among the disciples that brought peace, joy and tranquility to their hearts.

This raises a powerful question: What are we looking for during our troubles and bad circumstances? What changed the whole atmosphere of the disciples was not the answer of why this was happening, but rather the presence of Jesus among them. The great news for Christians today is that Jesus is not dead, but indeed He is rising. This means that in every single moment we face in life, He can be present to us through the Holy Spirit because He makes the Holy Spirit available to us. One of the roles of the spirit is the role of a consoler. This made and continues to make a big difference for the disciples who were locked inside of the room during Jesus' death and for us today. Several times in the gospel of John we read of Jesus telling the disciples

---

[8] Archibald Thomas Robertson, *Word Pictures in the New Testament John and Hebrews V* (Nashville: Broad Man Press: 1932), 313.

about the Holy Spirit, but He had not yet given them access to the Holy Spirit. Therefore, it was normal for the disciples to feel fearful because they did not have access to a deeper connection with God at that time nor the ability to feel His presence in the midst of their fear. However, today we are able to have this deeper connection with God because the Holy Spirit is available to us.

What is controlling you? For me, it was those dark moments, those moments that lacked coherence. For the disciples it was the death of the Messiah, the one in whom they had put all their trust. However, what changed everything for the disciples was the presence of the resurrected Chris among them. What changed my atmosphere was the acknowledgment of Jesus' presence along the way with me in the midst of everything. To know that He is present with me and that I can be relaxed regardless of it all gives me comfort. I do not know what form of fear is holding you, nor do I want to know because I'm not the best one to resolve it. However, I am encouraging you to look and search for the right thing, which is not understanding why but more importantly acknowledging the presence of Jesus in the midst of it all.

As the biblical text continues, it demonstrates the impact of Jesus' presence in the atmosphere of the disciples. As the text tells us, the disciples became overjoyed. Could it be that the celebration on that day was similar to how sports fans have behaved over the past decades? Or could it be that the second time Jesus said, *"Peace be with you"* He was encouraging them to relax. In other words, relax guys, keep the emotions down, there is bigger work out there. Jesus' presence shifted a room full of fear to an overjoyed place.

Eirene, tranquility was brought to the disciples in such a way that it not only brought peace but brought peace and joy in an overloaded measure - *the power of the presence of Christ.*

While their fear turned to joy, Jesus commanded them to go to the world like He himself was sent to this world by His Father. It is written in the text in this way: *"As the Father has sent me, I am sending you"* (John 20:21b NIV). In other words, He said not to stay inside of the room, but to go fulfill the same calling He had had from the Father to do in this world.

It is quite interesting to think that Jesus knew well enough that the disciples were overcome by the fear of the outside world. Yet Jesus commissioned the disciples to go out into the world. The first thing that this action required was to overcome the fear that they had concerning what lay out there in the world: the fear of the unknown.

It is important to ask: What did Jesus commission the disciples and us to do in the world? John, known as the Beloved disciple, is credited as the author of this gospel. One of John's primary foci on Jesus is exploring the manifestation of love, character and nature of the Father in Jesus' life. In other words, John set Jesus as the perfect example of what the Father is like. Not that Jesus is the Father, but rather the author projected the Trinity in a very philosophical and paradoxical way. He projected the differences that exist in each person of the Trinity and the specific role that each one plays. He also projected them as one, which makes it paradoxical. Therefore, in this commission from Jesus and in light of the author (the Beloved disciple), Jesus commanded the disciples and us today to do His primary work on earth. He did not command us to die on the cross but to reveal God to others, which begins through our way of living.

What Jesus commanded the disciples and us to do today is as follows: "As the Father had sent me to reveal him in this world, in the same way I'm sending you." Remember that those He first commissioned were those disciples who had hidden themselves in a small room because of fear. He called them to step out from the small room of fear, in the same way He is calling us to step out from our small circle of fear and reveal Him in this world.

It is interesting to observe that when Jesus told them that He knew well enough that they were not perfect. He also knew that through this step, they would grow spiritually and become more like Him. From our human understanding, we often see ourselves not good enough to be sent by God.

The text tells us that after Jesus commissioned the disciples, He breathed on them and told them *"Receive the Holy Spirit."* In other words, He said, I will not let you guys go like that, so receive the Holy Spirit. Jesus gave it to them but left it up to them to receive it. It is very difficult to receive anything that is given to us without the action of us reaching out to receive it. The Holy Spirit was not only made available to the disciples but He was also made available to us today. After giving them the Holy Spirit, He then gave them power over forgiveness.

Although I'm not diving into the significance of each action in that section, I have always been curious to understand why Christ gave them power over that specific discipline. Was it because Jesus knew the bitterness that the disciples had against some of the Jewish leaders or the bitterness, they had towards those who had crucified Him?

Thomas

Thomas is often defined as a doubting Thomas; in fact, we have traditionally referred to him as the doubting one. We even call someone who doubts a "doubting Thomas." In this portion, we read of Thomas' unbelief that Jesus was resurrected from the dead. Despite his unbelief, one must not forget that Thomas was a person with conviction who was willing to die with the Lord (John 11: 16 NRSV).

What many do not realize in this portion is that, like all the other disciples, Thomas was broken and sad, as others had been before. In the first appearance of Jesus to his disciples Thomas was not present when Jesus found them in fear. So, as the other disciples were broken before Jesus' appearance to them, Thomas too was broken before His appearance to him. That does not mean that the reaction of Thomas was good, because it would have been better for Thomas to believe the disciples in the first place. In fact, a week later the biblical text tells us that Jesus appeared to his disciples and Thomas was included. And Jesus said to Thomas, *"Blessed are those who have not seen and yet have believed"* (John 20: 29 NIV). However, it is important to have a look at what shook Thomas' belief. It was not common in those days, neither in our day for a person who died to be raised from the dead. Although Thomas might have been there or heard that Jesus raised Lazarus from the dead, the news of Jesus' resurrection sounded humanly impossible to Thomas. Now like Thomas, how often do we doubt God's capability? Not just what we believe to be humanly impossible, but with what are very simple difficulties.

What changed the position of Thomas and his unbelief was simply the presence of Jesus. The text tells us that Jesus showed proof to Thomas and commanded him to believe. Thomas faced what he thought was impossible and saw that it was possible. Then Thomas confessed and said, *"My Lord and My God."* What Thomas experienced was only God himself who made it possible and the only words that Thomas could use to describe what was real for him was *"My Lord and My God."* Like Thomas, we fail and we lose hope even after our conviction or willingness to follow Him. However, the most important thing in the midst of it all is the presence of the Holy Spirit because we can be relaxed and be at peace as long as we remain and abide in Christ.

Fear and doubt should not control our lives, nor should they hold us in hiding from revealing the great news. In the midst of our fear and lack of understanding, there is no greater thing to look for than the presence of Jesus. The power of Jesus' resurrection was made known to the disciples and Thomas at the moment they saw Him. It is unbelievable and not quite coherent the power of the presence of Christ unless you have experienced it. Jesus overcame death and through this victory we are able to overcome fear and bad circumstances.

Let's end with a prayer

Numerous times we face doubt, and this always ends up creating fear and insecurity in our life.
Help us, to be at peace and relax
Because our trust is found in no one else but you Lord

We can go hide wherever we think, but
only in you, there is true peace.
Help us to keep on abiding in your peace, God.
In the name of your precious son Jesus Christ we pray, Amen.

Chapter Five

Children as a Model

At least for the first decade of the 21st century, models are one of the things that have had a great impact on our society either in a positive or negative sense. A model is someone that many people look up to and that person influences how we live, talk, think and behave. For example, one of the people who had great influence during the early years of the 21st century was Michael Jackson. People often imitated the way he danced, talked and even dressed.

The majority of time if not all the time, the idea is for us to be a positive influence on children. To be a person they can look up to and imitate. It is a wonderful idea to be a positive influence for children. As a matter of fact, children today are the next generation and what we do today will influence how they will lead and how they will live their lives. However, in this chapter I'm switching things around and presenting things with a different perspective.

During the spring semester of 2017, I had a wonderful class with an outstanding professor. This class was servant leadership and it became my favorite leadership class in school. Near the end of the semester I asked my professor for an internship with kids and, luckily, they were looking for interns. During my internship I had the wonderful and powerful experience of working for four days at a summer camp. I had the chance to be engaged in dialogue with numerous kids and to observe all of them each day. I learned numerous things, but one specific thing I learned from the kids that impacted my spiritual life was how to live a faithful life as a Christian and to enjoy it on the same level that these kids enjoy and live life.

Many of the kids that I talked to at that camp were going through some hard times. It was not that they were unaware of the difficulties they were facing. Even with that knowledge they still enjoyed their lives to the fullest. Living life does not mean surviving, but to actually live it in a happy mood. To live life as a Christian is not to enjoy the pleasure of this world; it is to feel relaxed. It is not to be worried or frustrated by problems, but to fully enjoy faith regardless of the un-comfortability. It is to be at peace in troubles. It is a level or a mindset of trusting and dependency on God at all times.

When I engaged deeper in the reflection of enjoying and living life like little children, I understood that it was not only because of the atmosphere of summer camp that made the kids happy. In other words, kids are not only happy when they are at summer camp. As I was reflecting back on my own experience with kids, either in poor places in Haiti or in wealthy places. I observe how kids live and enjoy life at all time and in all circumstances. In many poor places where many of them don't have access to three good meals a day or even two good ones a day, the kids are still happy and enjoy life to its fullest. I had the privileged to be involved with kids in some poor places and I can honestly say that many of the kids did not like the environment they were in but they still enjoyed and lived life. In places where there is more financial security, kids face different troubles such as family divorce and they do not like it either, but they still enjoy and live life to the fullest.

Ernesto's Life

Soon after I got baptized in 2012, I became involved in the children's ministry at a church in Pernier, Port-au-Prince, Haiti. When I entered the ministry, there were not a lot of kids. There was an average of fifteen to twenty kids on Sundays. The ministry later grew three to four times larger in less than two years. One of my goals in this ministry was to get to know each child on a personal level. Not simply to know their names, but to understand their lives and their families. With this mindset I was able to connect with each child individually. One of the children who shocked me and who sets a great example to use for this discussion is Ernesto.

Ernesto was very young when he lost his father. He grew up very poor with his mother and his little sister. Ernesto was very protective of his family and became a little aggressive with anyone who annoyed his sister. Many perceived him as a kid that wasn't smart. Ernesto understood the conditions of his family life and was always willing to share what he had saved with his sister. When Ernesto had a cookie, his first thought was whether his sister had a cookie and whether he should save part of it for her. A lucky day for Ernesto would probably include three good meals, because a typical family like his would probably have a cup of coffee with some bread in the morning and something else for dinner in the afternoon. Ernesto had no video games, no bicycle nor any other games. However, Ernesto was one of the happiest and most energetic kids I have ever ministered to.

I knew him when he was about seven or eight years old. Ernesto was always happy. Although, he understood that his mom did not have much, it did not prevent him from being happy. Ernesto was always willing to help, to contribute and to engage in stuff. His environment was full of poverty, but his mind and heart were full of joy. Ernesto is a model who shows me how to keep living. For Ernesto, yes there were many difficulties in life, but they do not define what his mood should be. Ernesto would always volunteer himself to do the prayer in the children's services and in his prayers you could identify that this was a child that trusted and committed to his heavenly Father. Yes, there were many struggles for Ernesto during that time, but he always knew that he was not alone in life, that God was with him. Ernesto has been dependent on God and has lived each day as though each one was a celebration day. Sometimes, it is important to look at children and ask ourselves: "Are we truly living?" A stressful, overwhelmed and sad life is not a good life.

To live and enjoy a faithful life as a Christian is not about not fighting for social justice or against other problems that surround us. Nor does it depend on the present moment being perfect or that we accept everything and give up fighting for change. However, it is to understand the current reality and to actually live and enjoy life in the midst of it. There are two things that we can learn from little kids: first and foremost, it is the idea of being dependent and trusting and the second is to move on (to move forward).

Dependency and Trusting

A child does not worry much about the future. Depending on the age of the child, the child might not even worry about what he/she will eat tomorrow. Children are totally dependent on their parents or the one who is in charge of them. Often, we adults try to control everything as though we did not have a heavenly Father to provide the answers. In the Lord's prayer, Jesus taught His disciples to say "Give us this day our daily bread" (Matthew 6:11). In other words, give us today's meal. To not be too concerned about tomorrow or the future but simply think about today. Yes, it is important to save for tomorrow, but there is no reason to be overwhelmed by current issues or the future.

In this world, as we mature we become more independent and responsible. However, in the Christian spiritual world, as one matures spiritually the more that person becomes dependent on God and the more that person invites God into his or her decision-making.

Move on

A little child was playing with his friends. He was running with them and while he was running he fell down and started to cry. As soon as he started to cry, he ran into his father's arms. His father held him for a little while and shook him in a way that would help the little child to stop crying. After he stopped crying, the child continued playing with his friends. Yes, the kid fell down. Yes, it was a little painful for the kid. However, the kid moved on and returned to play with his friends. The struggle in many people's lives is to move on. Often, we are stuck in a single memory from the past and we keep complaining and crying over that one painful incident. I'm not saying that crying is bad nor am I saying that we should get over everything easily. There are certain things that will take time, such as the loss of a loved one or the loss of someone dear to us. However, there are countless painful or sad things that we should move on from easily. Unlike a little child, we need to learn from our mistakes. However, similar to a small child we need to run into the arms of the Lord and move on from our pain and sadness. Run to our Heavenly Father's arms for all issues, no matter how big or how small.

When they disciples asked Jesus how should we pray? The first two words that Jesus said in the prayer was "Our Father." One problem is that depending on which culture you come from or which family you grow up in, you might attach the wrong meaning or definition to what is a good father. However, our heavenly Father is different. He is one that we can run to at all times and in any circumstance. Therefore, one need to enjoy his relationship with the heavenly Father by running to His arms at all time, in all circumstances.

CHAPTER SIX

PRINCIPLES FOR JOY

Writing this book has been a great spiritual journey for me. I have grown in many different ways and now understand different things in a better way. In my first outline of the book I did not include this chapter. However, later on I felt compelled to include a chapter about some important principles that are needed for one to live a peaceful and relaxing life. These principles do not bring peace in themselves, but they are very important concepts for one to understand to live a peaceful life. It is important to find a good balance between the concepts and the way we live our life.

"Make good friends and value family but put your ultimate trust in God alone"

We all are called to live in harmony and fellowship with others although we recognize our differences. Some of us have a small group of friends and family, while others have a very big group of friends. No matter how big or small the circle is, it is important to keep that circle healthy.

Everyone needs other people, even the most independent person needs people. We are called to live in community and fellowship with one another. In fact, there are certain problems we experience that are impossible to handle alone. It is important to share them with someone close to you. When we do so the problems seem smaller and more manageable. When our relationship is right with others, we are in a sense healthier.

Relationships do matter and they are at the core of the Christian foundation. In fact, Jesus defined our relationship with God as a relationship between a father and a son. And Jesus also said *to "Love the Lord your God with all your heart and with all your soul and with all your strength and with all your mind; and, Love your neighbor as yourself."* (Luke 10:27 NIV). In this verse, we see that we are not simply called to love God, but also to love our neighbor. In other words, the harmony is not simply between us and God; we need to live in harmony with our neighbor. Jesus himself projects the difference in loving God and loving our neighbor. We should focus on God with our heart, soul, strength and mind, but we love our neighbor as we love ourselves. It does not say to put your ultimate trust in your neighbor, but to treat your neighbor in the same way you would treat yourself.

It is important to have good friends and to truly value your family, but it is important to understand that none of your friends or family members is God. Therefore, it is imperative to put God first in your life. Not your mother, nor your wife or husband, nor your children, but God alone. There are circumstances that you may find yourself in where none of the people you care about are present, but you know that God will always be there for you. Or you can have everyone present with you, but if God is not with you, you are missing the most important thing. Make good friends and value family but put your ultimate trust in God alone. People will disappoint, but God does not.

"Be free from the love of money and from the riches of this earth"

I am not against money nor do I believe that money is evil. In fact, I ask a question for those who say that money is evil. Why do we have offerings in church services? In addition, the same group that declares money is evil also uses money to purchase things. I am not against money nor am I against those who have great financial success. However, there is a danger in living only for money or for the riches on this earth. Neither money nor other riches of this earth are eternal. Therefore, it is important to understand the difference between *living in* riches and *living for* riches.

When someone lives for riches, he or she tends to be the slave of riches. One other problem with living for riches is that those who live for riches are never satisfied; they want more and more. If one day they lose some of their possessions, they panic because that is what they were living for.

"Love people, serve people, be kind and respectful to everyone, but do not live for people's approval"

Certain criticism is very important; in fact, criticism is needed for us to improve. However, what ends up happening is that many people live their life to gain approval from others. They worry about what people think and say about them. In other words, they are living with the purpose of pleasing those around them. It is sad because a person who is trying to please people is like someone who is trying to take all the water out of the ocean. It is impossible to take every drop of water out of the ocean and in the same way it is impossible to please everyone. It is important to be kind, respectful and to serve everyone around you. However, being kind, respectful and serving others are not the same as pleasing everyone.

Living for someone's approval often comes from low self-esteem or the lack of confidence in oneself. The problem this creates is that you find yourself in a place where you are not fully stable in your own self-identity. You live to please others, but not to be you. Even if we are looking at pleasing people in a ministerial way, it will create the conflict between the will of God and pleasing others. Christ did the will of God, but He did not live to please people. In fact, many people did not appreciate some of Christ's sermons or teachings. The challenge is to find a balance between loving others, serving others and being the person you really are.

I started this section talking about the importance of certain criticism. It is important to acknowledge that there are at least two types of criticism: constructive criticism and destructive criticism. Even though we need criticism and advice, we must do our best to put ourselves in a place where we can discern the difference between the two. At a very young age I established two different categories for criticism and advice, so every time I hear criticism or advice I try to evaluate which category it fits into. Does the person delivering the criticism know what he or she is talking about? And are they offering the criticism out of love or out of envy?

You will meet many people who criticize you, but they do not understand where you are or the strategy you are implementing. In other words, these people do not understand your current reality. However, depending on the one who's giving you advice or criticism you can still learn something from them. Understand the spirit of criticism. Often people criticize you not because what you are doing is wrong, but simply because they wish they were in your place. However, some great people will give you good criticism and useful advice out of love. (I have met many great people who do that.) Live for God and find your identity in Him, but do not live to please others.

"Do not compare yourself to others and understand that you are a unique creature of God"

It is easy and common for anybody to compare himself or herself to someone else. It is something we all do. However, the practice of comparing oneself to another person often times creates low self-esteem. When people compare themselves to someone else, they often feel inferior when they see that the other person is better at something than they are. This can create jealousy, which could lead them to do something bad to the other person.

It is important to understand that we are all not as gifted at the same things. The fact that someone is better in certain things does not actually mean that we are inferior to the other person. We all have our strengths and weaknesses in life. Therefore, it is important to understand that we are all different and are all special in our own capacity.

It is good to acknowledge someone else's gifts and learn from that person, but it is a bad habit to compare oneself to another person. People are different and they have their own abilities which are shaped and influenced from past experiences. Unfortunately, the majority of us, if not all of us, struggle with self-comparison. The more we can free ourselves from self-comparison the easier it we will be to have peace within. It is important for each person to understand that they are unique and special in Christ. In fact, our different gifts, approaches, characteristics and understanding complete the bigger picture.

"Be grateful and thankful for even the little things"

Sadly, many people see happiness and contentment as a materialistic goal to reach in life. Therefore, that mentality prevents people from living a happy life. Unfortunately, happiness is not based on the amount of material possessions one accumulates. Often, we focus on reaching a certain level of wealth and we forget to be grateful for the little things we have the privilege of possessing.

We do not find contentment in the things we have access to, but we do find contentment when we appreciate these things. We express our appreciation by being grateful and thankful. We are all blessed and are graciously gifted with many things. Many times, we make lists of what we want or what we need, but we rarely make a list of what we are grateful for. Seeing, talking, laughing, walking, eating, breathing and going to the restroom are things we should be grateful for. Even if one might have access to just few of these things, be grateful for them.

My maternal grandma went through many difficulties in her life, yet she was one of the happiest women I have ever known. In spite of those difficulties in her life, she was essentially a happy person who always danced. One of the principles in her life that kept her happy was that she was always grateful and thankful for everything she had. My grandma and my mom's stepdad (grandpa) were considered one of the most joyful couples in the community they lived in, but they did not have a car or have the nicest house in their neighborhood. Yet they were grateful and thankful for even the smallest of things you could imagine.

Learn from your past, but do not let bad experiences in the past control your future

We all have a history and in each story there are some bad experiences. Some people's stories are sadder than someone else's. (This is not a comparison to show that someone is better, it is simply the reality.) My mom loved to say that "It is always better to prevent yourself from a sad and shameful experience." Unfortunately, some of us already have had bad experiences and we cannot go back to the past and change them. Since we cannot change those bad memories, we should not allow those bad experiences in the past to control our future. We must learn from them but learning from them does not mean to keep blaming oneself.

In the chapter on forgiveness I talked about the freedom in forgiving others. Sadly, many people can forgive others, but are unable to forgive themselves and accept that the

Lord forgave them. We often allow our past to hold us inside of a cage. When we are inside of that cage there is no way we can find peace or joy unless we are willing to set ourselves free. And the way to set ourselves free is through an act of repentance and confession to God. It is stated in 1 John 1:9, *"If we confess our sins, he is faithful and just to forgive us our sins and to cleanse us from all unrighteousness."* When God forgives, He does not hold on to the memory. If God forgives us, why shouldn't we learn to forgive ourselves? Let the past be the past, learn from the past and act in ways that won't create regrets in the future.

"Although not everything in life is coherent, it should not bring trouble to your life"

"Keep on trusting Christ"

We all in a sense want to find the answer to the question why. We love to understand things, and this is good. However, we are very limited beings and when we cannot answer certain questions in life, we often feel lost, frustrated and not in control. Some of us have been trying to answer a few questions while some of us will face questions in which we will never find the answers and we have to accept that this is part of the paradox of life.

It is important to accept that we are very limited beings. There are many things that go beyond our human capacity and reality that we cannot explain or will ever be able to explain. For example, the story of creation in the book of Genesis is one that is impossible to explain—how God made creation with words. God said, *"Let there be light, and there was light."* (Genesis 1: 3 NIV). There are countless other things that God created through words in the creation that are inexplicable. However, one of the reasons why we cannot understand nor explain it is because we do not really have an understanding of perfection nor have any of us ever made something perfect. Not only what God said were made in perfection, but His words had the power to create them. There are countless other examples of things that go beyond our imagination and comprehension, such as the Israelites in the Red Sea or God's love for humanity.

It all proves that we are limited beings; we do not understand everything, and we will never be able to. However, even if we cannot understand everything, especially the tragedies in life, it does not mean that we should be overwhelmed by them. The human mind cannot explain everything, but believing in Christ helps us to navigate all of these things. Do not be troubled by what you cannot understand.

CHAPTER SEVEN

GOD'S WILL IN YOUR PERSONAL LIFE

Discovering God's will for your life or discovering what God wants you to do next can be very stressful. It is something that we all face regardless of our age or where we are in life. Many young adults who are going to college do not have a clear purpose for their life or have not yet discovered their life purpose. Many college graduates also are trying to find God's will. Even many people who are getting close to retirement wonder what is waiting for them in the next stage of their life. These are just a few examples to show that different people in different stages of life wonder about God's will. It is always good for someone to identify God's good will for his or her life. Although this is very important, we should not be overwhelmed when it is difficult to understand or to discover God's good will in life.

From the onset I want to apologize for not starting with the favorite verse of many Christians on this topic of God's will: "*For I know the plans I have for you, declares the Lord, plans to prosper you and not to harm you, plans to give you hope and a future*" (Jeremiah 29:11). Like all others, I strongly believe that God wants the very best for everyone.

My problem is our understanding of God's good plan; in other words, how we interpret it. I have grown up listening to many preachers define God's good plan for someone or prosperity for someone as the ability to accumulate material possessions, not being sick and for everything to go well. Yet if this is God's good will or the meaning of God's good will for everyone, it makes me wonder where God's good will is for the homeless? and the poor in Africa and in Haiti? Or even more so, where was God's good will for the poor man named Lazarus in Luke chapter 16 verses 19 to 31? I strongly believe in God's good will for everyone, but I also often question our understanding of His good will. Yes, God has a good plan for humanity and for every single one, but this good will might be very much different from how we understand it or want it to be.

I wish I could, but sadly I cannot, define the exact will of God for everyone who is reading this chapter. I wish I could say that you will be a pastor, a Moses who will deliver his people or an Esther, but this would have been very manipulative of me. One of the puzzles around finding God's will for our life is the way we value success. The one in power is often considered to be the successful one. But we often forget that the one who is not seen is equally important. For example, inside of the church we value the pastors as the great servants who are fulfilling God's call. Yet there are also countless unseen great people serving in the church who are also fulfilling God's will.

When you think of God's good will for your life, what do you think of? What position do you see yourself in or what role do you see yourself playing?

It is good to reflect on these questions because

sometimes we just see doing things that are seen on the macro level as accomplishing God's will. We often forget that the little things we are doing are very important and have a great impact. Susanna Wesley, the mother of John Wesley, had nineteen children and she invested at least one hour every week in each child.[9] It was a time for her to engage in spiritual dialog with them. She was in charge of their education and she instilled "a sense of Christian Destiny into each of her children."[10] Two of her children had a great influence in the 18th century, and their work continues to be relevant to this day. My point is not to say that all women are called to stay home and take care of their babies and children, but it is to show that sometimes those unseen actions we do have a great impact and are very important. This helps to understand that it is not only a preacher, a teacher or someone visibly involved in a project who is fulfilling God's will, but even one who is involved in something that is unseen is also fulfilling God's will.

Discovering God's Will

How do we discover God's will? It is important to begin by emphasizing that there are often two main streams of thought. One stream supports predestination, which believes that it all has been planned and scheduled. This

---

[9] "Susanna Wesley: Mother of Methodism." YouTube. United Methodist Videos. April 07, 2016. Accessed May 26, 2018. https://www.youtube.com/watch?v=Zpi1OJ5LiVY.

[10] "16 House Rules by Susannah Wesley (John Wesley's Mom) Raising godly children." May 08, 2016, accessed May 26, 2018. http://www.raisinggodlychildren.org/2011/03/16-house-rules-by-susannah-wesley-john-wesleys-mom.html.

means that the destiny of everyone has already been selected and our actions are simply a fulfillment of what has been scheduled to take place. For this stream it is God in action in all circumstances because it was all predestinated. People who have this type of belief struggle whenever they are explaining human actions that are evil. At the beginning of 2018 there were many school shootings in the United States. It would be horrible to say that God is behind these horrific actions and that He had ordained and scheduled them to take place.

It is also important to acknowledge that sometimes God does things, or He predestinates certain things. However, we must also be able to differentiate between God all-knowing and God doings. It is important to remember that we all have free will when we do things from our own free will. It is different from God's will.

The other stream of thought sees God's will as a combination between God's good will and man's obedience. Another angle in that stream states that God blesses our actions if it is for the greater good, which means that God blesses our actions and the steps we take. The problem with this stream is that even though it acknowledges our contribution, which is good, it sometimes focusses less on the will of God. We must always focus on His calling and less on our decisions.

After reading about these two streams of thought, it is more likely that each person will support one stream or will argue that this one is the good one and the other is not. I used to believe in the stream that acknowledges man's free will for two reasons. First, because many people who believed in the other stream in my country just spent days fasting, praying and asking when God was going to perform a miracle for them. They waited for that miracle without doing anything. They would say, "I'll sit down and wait on the Lord." The second reason was because of my grandmother. My grandmother took control of her life and moved forward. She started a business and God blessed her in many ways for her commitment and hard work.

Now, even though I mention both of these two streams and share my early beliefs, it is important to emphasize that both streams are in the Bible in a balanced way and our interpretation must also be balanced. However, arguing about which one is relevant to your life is not what is most important. What is important is understanding that in finding God's will in life is about grasping the ideology that we are all unique and every single one of us has a special mission, a unique purpose and calling in life. A person can make a list and name five to seven of his or her favorite bible characters. One conclusion this person will end with is that every single biblical character he or she had selected had a specific mission, purpose and calling. And all these differences were for the good of God's kingdom. Therefore, it is important to understand that we are all unique and God moves differently in every single one of us.

In the previous paragraph I mentioned that if one makes a list and names some of his or her favorite bible characters they would see that each person in the selection had a special mission, purpose and calling. However, one will also observe that they all shared a relationship with God. The Christian faith is a journey, the believer is called to walk with God, and live in harmony with Him through Christ. We often worry so much about the future and we end up forgetting to enjoy the present moment and forget to appreciate our special relationship with Him.

This took a long time for me to realize. I understood it when I was dating my wife Rachel O. Estinvil. I would think about how our future was going to play out so much that I would end up forgetting to enjoy the present moment. So often we obsess about the future and miss the opportunity to enjoy life at the present moment. This does not mean we should not think or plan for the future, but we should not let the future overwhelm us to the point that we forget to enjoy the present moment. In a relationship every single moment is important and worth enjoying in a peaceful way.

In our relationship with God through Christ there are seven qualities that are needed in order for one to fulfil God's will. These seven qualities are patience, awareness, discernment, focus, determination, acceptance and willingness.

Patience: As Christ's followers, we often act like things have to be done in a rush or as soon as possible. However, God's calendar is very different and we need to be patient. Patience is a virtue that this generation needs.

Awareness: Often we forget that God speaks in many different ways and sometimes the answers are found in what we ignore or underestimate. Therefore, it is imperative to have self-awareness. To achieve self-awareness one must listen, observe, analyze and remain silent sometimes. Sometimes God speaks to us through a little child, via nature and in countless other ways.

Discernment: Sadly, when we become followers of Christ, we are not prevented from being tempted. With discernment we will be able to identify temptation. We need discernment to identify what is God's will and what is not His will.

Focus: Focus is the sense of visualization that keeps us on the plan's correct path. We can discover the vision and we can also have the plan, but if we do not focus we will not achieve the goal.

Determination: Not only do we need to focus, but we also need a sense of determination to achieve the goal. The focus helps us concentrate on the goal, but determination is what pushes us along the way to achieve the goal. It is the conviction to fight and achieve.

Acceptance: Acceptance might be my favorite quality because it brings openness for us to accept the reality. Not that we always agree with the reality, but we embrace it and understand that it helps us grow in Jesus Christ.

Willingness: We can ask God to help us, but we must first be willing to ask for His help. God does not force us. One needs to also demonstrate the desire to serve and help.

Three Important Tips

Whatever you do in life always make sure that it helps you transform to the likeness of Christ. In other words, you are spiritually growing and becoming more like Christ in your actions and personality. What you are involved in might help you become wiser, more patient, more loving, more dependent on God, or help you to become more like Christ.

The second tip is how it helps building the Kingdom of God or demonstrates to others God's love. Many people understand serving God as only serving within the church or being a missionary. However, we are all called to fulfill the great commission and we do not simply do it in missionary work or serving in the church. Even more so, it is something that needs to be fulfilled in whatever we do in life and wherever we are.

Do not be afraid to fail. A great thing is that God sees failure very differently than human beings see it. Whenever someone fails we are quick to judge them, quick to blame them and even quick to punish them. However, God sees failure differently. He sees it as a way for us to grow so we can learn from our mistakes. God knows perfectly that we are not perfect and that we will make mistakes, but He also provides the Holy Spirit for us. Do not be afraid to give things a try and pursue your sense of curiosity. The decisions you make today affect your future. (I will likely continue this discussion in this chapter in Volume 2.)

Chapter Eight

Peace in the Darkness

Darkness makes it very difficult for one to see what is around them. Not only does darkness make it difficult for one to see what is around, but it also makes it difficult for one to see the road to take or the path to go somewhere else. Darkness makes it difficult to understand and to be aware and this can cause confusion. It can also create fear, panic and make one lose hope.

Everyone faces or will face dark moments in life. Moments in which one cannot define where he or she is, moments where one can neither understand what is going on nor able to answer the question why. These moments can bring fear in our life and can also make one lose hope, but these moments in life don't define us. Darkness does not make you a new person although it can bring some changes in you. You are still the same person but in a different circumstance.

What should we do in these dark moments of life?

Instead of beginning with what we should do, let's begin with what we should not do. We should not allow these moments to define us or to make us neglect our identity.

These moments should not make us overreact or make one feel that suicide is the best and only option for peace. Conversely, these dark moments should make us experience God on a deeper level through faith and in a life following God's lesson.

There was a married man who had five children. He was going through a very dark moment in his life. He had several problems, one of which was the two-day shortage of food to feed his family. On the third day, the man went out and did his very best to bring some food or money back home, but he found neither a morsel of food nor even a dime. On his way back home while passing close to the sea not far from where he lived he considered suicide. Out of nowhere he heard a voice from within that told him to dive into the sea to take his life. He responded by asking, "What about my wife and children?" The response was, "A person that is dead has no children and no wife. Therefore, once you take your life the problem will be gone."

After a few seconds, the man began to pray: "Lord, I have no problem that my family and I die of starvation. However, it won't be from me giving up in life, but instead it is going to be me dying with complete trust in you. After the prayer the man continued walking home. Shortly after arriving home, two different people came to his house at different times. The first one came and purchased something for $60 from the man. The second person came right after and gave the man $100. Soon thereafter he was hired to do several jobs and contracts. What would be the story of this man today if that simple circumstance had brought an end to his life? What would be the future of his kids?

What should we do in the dark moments? The response

is to simply put into application these words of Jesus "*Come to me, all you who are weary and burdened, and I will give you rest. Take my yoke upon you and learn from me, for I am gentle and humble in heart, and you will find rest for your souls. For my yoke is easy and my burden is light*" (Matthew 11: 28-30 NIV). Within this passage there are three invitations from Jesus to those who are burnt out and overloaded by the circumstances of life. These three invitations are to go to Him, to take His yoke and to learn from Him. If a person accepts these three invitations, Jesus promises that this person will find rest in Him.

Even though Matthew was written for a Jewish audience and the style of the gospel proved it, Matthew shared the good news with everyone regardless of their race and their condition in life. (None are excluded from God's love manifested in Jesus Christ, even though it can be more difficult for some.) It is also important to acknowledge that Christ often leads to a sense of favoritism or more sensitivity towards those who are struggling. Yes, the dark moments are intense, but Christ is understanding (gentle), and humble in heart. Therefore, go to Him. How do we go to Him? The most common answer would be through prayer and praise of worship. But how do we pray when we do not know what to say or cannot put our reflection into words?

In the same way that it can be very difficult to see where to go in the darkness, it can also be very difficult for one to pray in a difficult moment. Prayer not within the context of a to-do checklist but prayer in the context of diving into a dialog with Jesus Christ. Clear sentences facilitate communication, but when there is nothing but tears and silence from you, it makes it difficult for another person to understand you. However, prayer is not all about how we formulate what we want to say; it is much more about the emotions and spirit that are deep within that cannot be put into words. In other words, it is mostly about the language of the heart. Even more, we can be confident that God understands this way of communication very well. Therefore, even when you do not know what to say and are simply crying, try to engage in prayer because God understands you very well.

The Christian faith is based on a collaboration between an individual and Christ. Jesus projects this clearly in this passage when He said, "*Take my yoke upon you.*" A yoke is something that is often put on the neck of two cows or more when they are pulling a heavy load. When two cows pull a load, it becomes easier to pull and it takes less time to reach the destination. The yoke also helps the animals to go in the same direction. If one goes right and the other left they will not move. They have to coordinate their movements to go in the same direction.

When the first audience received the words "Take my yoke upon you" it was an invitation not to live under the stress or law of tradition, but to live instead by his teachings and by believing in Him.[11] The application for those in the darkness is to not worry or become overwhelmed by reality, but instead to put our trust in Jesus and walk the difficult moment with Him. Through this act of submission not only are you not carrying the load alone, but Christ

---

[11] William Hendriksen, *New Testament Commentary on Matthew* (Grand Rapids: Baker Pub Group, 1978), 504-505.

accompanies you on your journey.[12] By taking the yoke of Jesus we experience freedom and rest from bondage.

And Jesus told them "*learn from me.*" In this phrase Jesus set himself on the level of a master, teacher and example for one to learn from. Through learning we become disciples with challenges that keep us learning and following Jesus.[13] For the early audience the challenge wasn't simply to take is yoke, but it was also a challenge for them to become humble, wise and to learn from Him. However, for a person in the darkness, it is difficult to learn when things are not clear, not coherent. How can one learn in these moments? For a Christian and a wise one, to live is to learn and as we are walking with Christ in these moments, we are learning as we are experiencing the compassion, love and faithfulness that are in Christ. The learning process is not like a student in a classroom, but instead it is a learning process that takes place through experience.

Jesus continues and elaborates on Himself when He said, "*For I am gentle and humble in heart.*" He was describing Himself as one that was different from many of the Jewish leaders at that time. He wasn't one to increase the burden or condemn others when things were difficult, but He was the one who is patient and kind (gentle). He is not legalistic nor does He set himself too high to relate to others, but instead He puts himself at your level and relates to you.

I was talking to a person who was in a very difficult time in her life and the person was thinking of making some very

---

[12] *The Interpreter's Bible, Vol. 7: New Testament Articles Matthew and Mark* (Nashville: Abingdon Press), 390.

[13] "Learn From Me," JW.ORG, December 15, 2001, accessed February 3, 2019, https://wol.jw.org/en/wol/d/r1/lp-e/2001923.

bad choices that would affect her parents' and her friends' lives. The person continuously said that no one in her family understood her nor did anyone else in her life. She was in the midst of a family crisis and I helped her to understand that maybe she didn't understand them either because the crisis affected all of them. She agreed with me. The lack of understanding can turn things upside down and can bring one to feeling more isolated or make the problem worse. In contrast, understanding opens doors for compassion and brings peace of mind.

There are moments in life when we do not see correctly nor understand things very well. But in these moments we abide more and more in Jesus and walk the journey with Him. We trust and follow the King of peace, the one who carries our burdens together with us. Not only does He do this, but He empathizes with us in all circumstances.

God Sometimes Communicates through Others

Frequently in our dark moments we long to hear God's voice, to feel Him and touch Him like we would do to someone that is physically present with us. And yet we forget to pay attention to how God communicates through His people. The argument is not to say that God is not a person or that one cannot hear Him like Moses or like countless others in the Bible. In contrast, it is important to be aware of the different ways that God communicates with us, especially through His ambassadors.

On December 4th, 2018, my lovely wife Rachel and I were feeling very excited as we made our way to the hospital for an ultrasound. Rachel was nine weeks pregnant and this was the day that we were going to see the baby, hear the heartbeat and announce the pregnancy to our parents. It's nearly impossible for me to describe the excitement and joy that we were feelings since a week before that day. The excitement continued as we drove to the hospital and waited in the hall for the ultrasound to take place.

We became overjoyed when we saw the baby on the ultrasound, but after a few seconds the nurse told us that she had to go find the doctor. I wasn't worried at all because I didn't understand anything, but my wife told me that she noticed that the baby wasn't moving. Then the doctor came and after a few minutes she told us that the size of the baby was correct but there was no heartbeat. The baby was nine weeks, but something went wrong and the baby died. In less than a minute I transitioned from lightness to darkness. I wished that I could have seen the light but couldn't. I wished that I could have understood but instead I was broken. I wished I could have heard one word from God, but instead silence was the melody of a long song. Not only was the news terrifying but looking at my lovely wife crying made it worse. I admired the honesty of the doctor, but I still wish she could have been more humane and could have expressed empathy.

My wife and I re-scheduled an ultrasound for the following Tuesday. From Tuesday the 4th of December till Saturday morning of the 8th, I thought that God had forsaken me in the darkness, but on Saturday I experienced God differently. On Saturday while we helped at an event, the children pastor hugged my wife and started to cry with her. She said to my wife, "I know your mom is not in the same state with you, but I want to be that mom to you and share all support." Immediately after hearing these words, I heard something else from within speak to me with the following words, "Instead of looking for My (God) presence physically, seek me in my ambassadors." Numerous times in sad circumstances we think that God is absent while God isn't absent at all. Instead His ambassadors are not fulfilling their duty. In order for the love of God and the spirit of God to reach out to others, this love needs to be embodied in the lives of Christ's ambassadors.

It is dangerous to think that you are alone in the darkness and left alone to handle everything by yourself. The first decision is to run to the Savior and the second decision is to surround yourself with people of God. (One of the ways to identify these people of God is to observe if they love, if they offer kindness and generosity and if they carry such qualities inside of them). Darkness is just part of the journey and we must embrace it. Even more, it is when we should put the invitations of Jesus' record in Matthew 11: 28-30 into practice.

When we allow Christ's ambassadors to be in our circle, we do not proceed on our journey alone.

It's useful to close this chapter with the following prayer.

The prayer of the blind!

We hear and see, but we don't understand anything, for things have gone far beyond our comprehension. We raise millions of questions and break the issue into many pieces, but still don't get how it works for our good. We are often stuck on the issues of right here and right now, but hardly understand where you're bringing us and how you're preparing us for the upcoming future. Oh Lord, please grant us wisdom and your spirit so we can understand better.

We are bold in our faith and certain in your love for us, but also broken from within. We see the need and see how we can help, but we are empty from within. Oh Lord, please grant us courage and your spirit so we can fight more.

We are desperate for change and unable to wait for peace. We hear about hope but are often overcome by the circumstances of today. Oh Lord, please grant us patience and your spirit so we can relax in life.

We constantly face others' wrong doing and other difficulties. Oh Lord, please grant us grace and your spirit so we can have self-control in life.

Oh Lord, help us to keep walking by faith though it might demand that we get comfortable with uncertainty whenever it comes to following your will. Help us to keep on meditating on your grace, goodness and faithfulness even when we hear nothing but silence. Guide us in the road that will help us transform to your likeness, though we might face hungry lions on the road. Teach us to fully live in your presence though we face many distractions daily. Keep us from falling unless it's the only way for us to grow. Amen!

CHAPTER NINE

SELF-CONTROL

Self-control has often been taught within the context of living a moral life and it has typically targeted young people to avoid immoral acts. Although this is a very important and crucial aspect, self-control is more than this. Self-control is needed in all parts of our life. Self-control is not simply integrated into our actions or our words, but it should be integrated into the emotional aspects of our life. Self-control is defined as the "control or restraint of oneself or one's actions, feelings, etc."[14] Even more, not only did God create us in His image, but He also created each one of us with the ability to control ourselves. The purpose of this chapter is to help us understand the importance of self-control, how it is integral to all aspects of our life, to help us build a spirit that fights to control the self even when it seems impossible and to connect us with the reality of how God wants us to have control over our self.

---

[14] "Self-control," Dictionary.com. Accessed October 11, 2018. https://www.dictionary.com/browse/self-control.

A Person without Self-control

In order for us to fully understand the importance of self-control, it is necessary to imagine a person without self-control. What is it like to have no self-control in life? What is the danger of not having self-control?

A person without self-control is like an empty plastic bag that is not attached to anything and the wind directs the plastic bag wherever the wind wants it to go. If the wind goes east, the plastic bag blows to the east and if the wind goes west, then the plastic bag is carried to the west. However, one of the saddest things is that the wind can direct the plastic bag to a tree where it gets stuck. Or the wind can carry the bag to countless other places where it ends up torn into shreds. The wind can also direct the plastic bag in the direction of a fire, where the plastic bag ends up burning. In this analogy, the empty plastic bag is a human being who lacks self-control. The wind can sometimes be life itself or circumstances in life, and for some others the wind can be the devil or temptations that someone faces in life.

The danger lies in the circumstances of life, in possible temptations, in seemingly random emotions or in the devil. They all move you and manipulate you as they wish. Your circumstances can often define your mood, and your emotions can influence your actions and easily guide you down the wrong path where the devil can play you like a toy. Therefore, it is crucial for a person to be emotionally balanced and to have self-control because without it you will not be well adjusted. The lack of self-control does not simply have a negative impact on someone; it also affects the ones close to this person. It can negatively affect where you live and even affect all of humanity. For example, a person who takes a gun and shoots into a public space creates a bad image for the shooter's family. Furthermore, this act affects society and humanity in a negative way.

All Aspects of Our Life

As I stated previously, self-control is integral in every single area of a person's life. Self-control is needed within the emotional aspect (how we handle our emotions), how we spend our money, how we behave, and the list could go on and on. Even though self-control needs to be an integral part of our life, it is important to emphasize that only Jesus had complete self-control of His life.

Although we might not have self-control in all the areas of our life, it does not give us permission to act irresponsibly and do whatever we want to do. The goal needs to be to develop a sense of awareness in the areas where we lack self-control and brings improvements in them.

The Battle of Gaining Self-control

It would be unreasonable of me to write about self-control and yet be out of touch with the reality of life. Since life often guides us to a place where it is very difficult to control one- self, it is crucial to recognize that there are numerous obstacles to achieving a sense of balance. It is important to ask if it is possible to always have control over oneself. If the answer is yes, what about those who suffer with addiction? What about those who have a mental problem? Are we strong enough on our own to overcome temptation, depression and the anxieties of life?

We all can agree that mental problems are very different from the other problems and should be addressed and treated by a professional. With respect to the other matters, it is very important to acknowledge that part of living involves fighting. Although life is a battle and sometimes, we might not have control over one or several parts of our life, we should continue to fight. No one can fully control what is coming, neither ceaseless pain nor constant disappointments. However, we can control the way we respond and at the end of the day we are responsible for all of our actions and decisions. Self-control is an ongoing battle.

Is self-control a contradiction message to Relax?

The message of self-control does not contradict the first chapter of *Relax*. The title refers to opening space for God. "To open space is to surrender the problem to God. It does not mean that we are ignorant of the problem," but we are opening up space for God to work within the circumstances. Self-control is the ability to control oneself. It is not the ability to control everything in life; rather it is the ability to achieve a balance and not to permit every little thing in life to upset us. Self-control does not contradict the message of *Relax;* it is actually part of the message. Furthermore, it encourages growth to become what God wants us to be.

The messages of Jesus and the apostles always challenge us to control our actions and reactions. It is important for one to recognize that we cannot handle everything on our own and we need to open space for God, but the spirit works together with us. In other words, to gain control over oneself as a Christian is something that takes place from both the will and the spirit. It is also important to acknowledge that some people can gain control of the self quickly, while others take a much longer period of time.

God wants us to be Mature in the Area Self-control

The calling is much more than escaping hell; it is an invitation to be transformed in the image of Christ. Jesus set the challenge as follows: "Be perfect, therefore, as your heavenly Father is perfect" (Matthew 5: 48). In this chapter Jesus elaborates on anger, adultery, divorce, swearing, retaliating and loving your enemies. In addressing these matters, He challenges how we respond. He gives us the responsibility to respond rather than blaming the other person. People cannot respond in these ways Jesus emphasizes in Matthew 5 if they are led by their own feelings. The challenge of being perfect is to be fully-grown, mature and brought to completion.[15] In other words, it is to be like Christ who revealed the Father to us. Sin has made us imperfect beings, and we are called to strive and grow in the likeness of Christ.

It is always fascinating to me when I read or think of the story of Jesus calming the storm: "*Then he got into the boat and his disciples followed him. Suddenly a furious storm came up on the lake, so that the waves swept over the boat. But Jesus was sleeping. The disciples went and woke him saying, "Lord, save us! We're going to drown!"* He replied, *"You of little faith, why are you so afraid?" Then he got up and rebuked the winds and the waves, and it was completely calm. The men were*

---

[15] Hendriksen, *New Testament Commentary*, 504-505.

*amazed and asked, "What kind of man is this? Even the winds and the waves obey him" (*Matthew 8:23-27)!

Traditionally this passage is used to highlight the power of Jesus to calm the weather. We often conclude that God is going to calm the storms in your life. This interpretation is not wrong at all. However, for a moment I want you to pause and reflect on Jesus in this story. It is often difficult for someone to sleep in an atmosphere that isn't quiet or peaceful, but within this passage we read that Jesus slept in the middle of a storm. It is important to mention that boats at this time in history were not as comfortable and safe as are our modern boats. Therefore, it is easy to imagine the impact of the waves soaking everyone and how danger constantly threatened the poorly constructed boats. In the midst of this treacherous storm when the boat was very shaky, Jesus was sleeping. Also consider that many of the disciples were skilled fisherman, yet they were afraid of the storm. But, Jesus continued to sleep.

Jesus was annoyed when He awoke from His sleep and heard His disciples complaining. It is often difficult to experience both the divinity and humanity of Jesus in one setting or action. However, in this passage we experience both at the same time. One of the things I have experienced in my short life is that people don't like to be disturbed when they are sleeping, and we see this same reaction in Jesus. However, we also experience His divinity, for Jesus was not surprised or unnerved by the weather. Who would wake up in the middle of storm in a boat on the water with big waves crashing all around and wouldn't get scared? Instead of Jesus being upset, He asked them why they were afraid. Jesus knew what was happening, but He couldn't understand why they were afraid of the storm. Now, it is important to reflect on why Jesus was not surprised and shocked.

I strongly believe that while deeply sleeping Jesus was aware of the storm and His belief in the Father ensured His safety. He was aware of the bad storm, but He was relaxing and didn't allow the circumstances to control Him. He slept in peace in the middle of the storm for He knew His security was in the Father. The sad thing is that the storm made the disciples forget where they were heading, and all of their anxiety took control of them. The disciples forgot who they were and who their leader was. How would the story be different if they disciples decided to rebuke the rain in the name of Jesus? Or how would the story be different if the disciples had followed their Master and fallen asleep?

Waking Jesus up can be considered the disciples' act of faith, for their hope was solely in Jesus. But Jesus described them as people of little faith. Were the disciples wrong to wake up Jesus? We can argue and put forth different ideologies. However, the problem was not that the disciples woke Jesus up, it was that they were anxious about the circumstance and the fear they felt. Numerous times in a storm we allow anxiety and stress to control us, and we forget who we are, our purpose and our destination in life. Can we try to be like Jesus in such circumstances? Though we are aware of the circumstances, can we try to be as relaxed as Jesus was and fall asleep?

Jesus knew His destiny, and He knew that the situation was not the end. He was secure and at ease because He knew that His Father was in control. God wants us to be in control of our emotions. He does not want us to be like the empty plastic bag that can be easily carried by the wind or a storm. He wants us to be able to overcome all circumstances and to live peacefully. The storm in your life can be very upsetting, but this shouldn't prevent you from being at peace. Even more, the storm shouldn't control your life or your emotions. Instead you should remember your mission, purpose in life and the person that is in control of your life. Circumstances and difficulties do not control the self and drive us crazy. However, we take a nap in the middle of the storm for we know Jesus is with us. Take a nap.

CHAPTER TEN

GOD IS SUFFICIENT

Nowadays, you do not need to be a refugee to look for a place to take refuge. We all are looking for a safe place. Many Christians in persecuted countries and many Christians in places that are vulnerable to natural disasters are looking for a peaceful place to take refuge. People who live in developed countries are also looking for a place where they can be safe, safe from a terrorist attack and from a public shooting.

As political tensions increase globally, everyone is searching for a place where they can feel safe. As incomprehensible and malicious leaders gain control of nuclear weapons and other types of weapons, many people find themselves living with insecurity. No one knows when or where the next attack will take place. In countries where selfish political leaders have inherited their power and property, they take their countries hostage. Their self-centered attitudes and actions promote fear and suffering. Many young people opt to leave their country or if they choose to stay they embrace the misery or mobilize to fight, while others engage in immoral acts to survive. Believe it or not, political leaders' decisions affect our society, economy and security either in a positive way or a negative way. Natural disasters are the other end of the spectrum. They create panic. With social media and television coverage, breaking news continuously invades our sense of safety. Right in the middle of this tension are selfish, arrogant and irrational humans like you and me who focus on our own self-interest. Some of us cannot get along with each other and our reluctance to try helps to nurture division among us. People who fail to recognize that our actions affect our environment are creating problems for future generations. Peace and cooperation seem to elude us.

When it comes to searching for peace many of us are, in a sense, refugees. If we would only take a break and look back in history, we would see that our struggles are not new. Throughout the history of humankind, we see the driven forces of fear, panic and tension. For example, in the early decades of the 20th century we fought two wars that killed millions of young men and civilians: World War I and World War II. During the 16th and the beginning of the 17th centuries there was the Protestant Reformation that created fear and resorted to violence. We can find numerous historic examples of fear, panic and tension. Thanks to God, the people of God can always take their refuge in Him, which has been illustrated throughout scriptures.

To me the Bible is not God. When we refer to scripture, we find many promises; we read about many historical events and learn countless lessons that help us grow spiritually. One of the historical readings that is relevant here is Psalm 46: *"God is our refuge and strength, an ever present help in trouble."* Many theologians refer to 2 Chronicles 32 as the background story of Psalm 46. It was a moment in the history of Jerusalem when a battle was taking place against the king of Assyria. At that time Assyria was a more powerful country than Jerusalem. Even though the Assyrian army was better equipped than the army of Jerusalem, King Hezekiah of Jerusalem told his people to "Be strong and courageous. Do not be afraid or discouraged because of the king of Assyria and the vast army with him, for there is a greater power with us than with him." King Hezekiah did not count on his own power or capacity, he took refuge in God.

The main idea in Psalms 46 is that God is sufficient. The author is proclaiming that God is sufficient in the midst of natural disaster, war or fighting between nations. The psalm proclaims that though the mountain might fall into the heart of the sea or a nation fights among them, those who take their refuge in God should not be afraid. Not only do we take our refuge in God, but we also find strength and peace in God.

Psalm 46 is a hymn of praise that proclaimed the faith of many people of God at a specific time. When we read Psalm 46, we read the testimony of many people of God who suffered difficulties, but these people did not handle these challenges on their own. Instead, they took their refuge in God. Their proclamation of faith is an inspiration to us today, that God is sufficient. And that we can take our refuge in God, even though the problems can look as big as a mountain or as strong as a storm. We should not worry, but simply take our refuge in God and if the Almighty, the God of Jacob and Abraham, the Creator, the Alpha and Omega is with us, why should we be troubled?

Psalm 46 is a very powerful psalm and well-known by many. It was a proclamation of faith by a group of people, at a particular time in history. And these people's proclamation of faith has helped countless others throughout history to trust and find their comfort in God. Many times, we look back in history, but we do not really grasp the idea that it was different then than it is today. That it is a historical moment and the way we face a situation leaves an example for the next generation. For the people in Jerusalem during King Hezekiah's reign, God was their refuge and strength. They proclaimed so and took their refuge in God. They started seeing God's power through victory. My question to you is what's your proclamation of faith?

I'm inviting you to put the psalm in your own words and make it become your proclamation of faith. You can do so by filling in the blanks with your own words or write them down on another piece of paper. There is no right or wrong way to do it. Put it in your own words and make it your proclamation of faith.

1 God is my .... and ...., an ever-
present .... in ....
2 Therefore I will not ...., though ....
and .... the heart of ....,
3 though it's .... and ....
and .... with ....
4 There is a .... whose .... make glad the city
of God, the holy place where the Most High dwells.
5 God is within her, she will ....;
God will ....

6 ...., ... he
lifts his voice, the earth melts.
7 The Lord Almighty is with me; the
God of .... is our fortress.
8 Come and see what the Lord has done,
the ....
9 He makes wars cease, to the ends of the earth. He
breaks .... and ....; he ....
10 He says, "Be still, and know that I am God; I will be
exalted among the nations, I will be exalted in the earth."
11 The Lord Almighty is with me; the
God of .... is my fortress.

PART TWO

ON A COLLECTIVE LEVEL

CHAPTER ELEVEN

ETHICAL DISAGREEMENT

Throughout history there have always been ethical crises that have created numerous problems in society. For example, throughout the 19th century there were diverse ethical issues being discussed: women's rights, slavery, racial discrimination and countless others. Every society faces different ethical issues and we cannot stop the speeding train of changing times. Although we cannot stop the train, we can prevent some damage. My concern is that in every ethical conflict there has been a group of people who are victimized. I'm asking, "How can we peacefully and rationally discuss these ethical disagreements?"

From the beginning I need to acknowledge that when we address ethical issues especially within Christianity there have always been two main streams of thought: conservative Christians and liberal Christians. In such a dialogue we need the participation of both streams. My position is not to determine if an ethical dilemma is right or wrong or to change something from being morally wrong to become morally right. We can neither ignore the existence of right and wrong nor can we ignore the need for positive change in our society today. My objective is not to lower the standard; in fact, Jesus raised the standard. The Old Testament was about loving your neighbor and hating your enemy. Jesus switched things around and said to love your enemy (Matthew 5:43-44). I'm not focusing on lowering the standard but gaining a better sense of understanding and acting in a way that will help others find peace amid ethical disagreement and that will impact many to live a transformational life.

This chapter is a dialogue that will never end since everyone has an important perspective about ethical issues. Although I was not able to interview everyone, I'll share the ideas of a few people I interviewed on the idea of living peacefully when there are ethical disagreements.

Professor Amos Gabriel

Professor Amos Gabriel is one of the people I interviewed in the chapter of *A Peaceful Ministry*. For him, one of the main issues when talking about ethics is that leaders and Christians often take a legalistic approach. In other words, he believes that instead of responding in a Christ-like way, we are quick to blame and condemn. Professor Amos believes that if Jesus saw things in a legalistic or a black and white way then the woman who was caught in adultery would have been put to death by Jesus. He points out that the woman was caught in a sinful act and Jesus told her to *"Go now and leave your life of sin"* (John 8: 11b). However, Jesus did not use her failure to condemn her, but offered her another opportunity. Professor Amos suggests that there is the need for compassion and willingness to understand, even though there might be complete disagreement.

Professor Amos supported his argument about the *willingness to understand* with a real-life story that happened several years ago when he was in a church leadership position. The story was about an eighteen-year-old girl who was rumored to be spending time with a married man. The clergy of the church invited the young lady to a meeting at which time they were ready to stop her from participating in all church-related activities. They were ready to condemn her. (This is a common practice of several churches in certain places.) When many members of the clergy team were close to suspending her from all church activities, Professor Amos asked the young lady why she was going out with the married man. She responded that her mother had eight children and she was the oldest. She was in ninth grade and her dream was to finish school. However, her mom did not have enough money to support her and that she became involved with the married man for financial support. For Amos, yes, the young lady did something wrong. However, wouldn't it be better if many in the clergy tried to understand her and help her fight the struggle instead of judging her? It would have been a more effective approach. For Professor Amos, a better option would have been to settle the ethical disagreement in a peaceful way, compassionately and with a willingness to understand.[16]

---

[16] Amos Gabriel, *Interview by Mardochee Estinvil*, San Antonio, February 2018.

Dr. Mario Ramos

I interviewed Dr. Ramos. He is a full-time professor at Baptist University of the Americas. He teaches several classes, including Biblical Ethics, Biblical Interpretation, Faith- walking. He has several years of experience in ministry as well. During the interview Dr. Ramos offered two reasons why we often cannot be at peace when there is an ethical disagreement: the issue of self-differentiation and the absence of inner peace.

When someone does not have a good level or balance of self-differentiation that person has difficulty separating their thinking from their emotions. That person will have difficulty seeing both sides of an argument or understanding both perspectives. This can cause one to act and react and even overreact during difficult times. It is important for a person to be able to separate their thinking from their emotions.

Not many people have an inner peace. This is very important because inner peace brings stability and a balance to our life. Numerous times those who do not have inner peace have trouble finding their identity in Christ, which can create low self-esteem. It is important to understand that the way people see themselves will affect how they behave toward others. When we have inner peace, we have the ability to make decisions without diminishing the value of someone else. Often our frustration affects our relationships with others.

Part of the solution that Dr. Ramos suggested is to preach the Gospel to ourselves every day and reflect on the following themes: how much we are loved, in Christ we are enough, how can I love others and be forgiving without devaluing anyone. It is also important to focus on what is best for the Kingdom of God.[17]

Dr. Rick McClatchy

I also had the privilege to interview Dr. McClatchy. Dr. McClatchy served as a pastor at four different churches, and he has taught as an adjunct professor at several universities and seminaries. He has been serving in several capacities in ministry especially within the cooperative Baptist fellowship.

Interesting to me was that Dr. McClatchy noted that many denominations in Christianity use the same bible, but they are unable to reach an agreement. He suggested that we need to learn to be different and not to be divided. In other words, we can disagree, but we shouldn't be divided because of our disagreement.

Dr. McClatchy also emphasized that we need to understand that we are all made in the image of God. Because we are all made in the image of God, there is the divine image of God in all of us. Once we start seeing it this way it challenges how we act towards each other. Since we are all made in the image of God, everyone should be treated with respect and love. In our actions and decisions we must make sure that we promote peace and harmony and that we do not disvalue or diminish others.[18]

---

[17] Mario Ramos, Interview by Mardochee Estinvil, San Antonio, March 29, 2018.

[18] Rick McClatchy, Interview by Mardochee Estinvil, San Antonio, March 29, 2018.

Mardochee Estinvil

The concept of ethics deals with moral principles. However, I do not want to engage in what is morally right and wrong in this chapter. Neither do I want to ignore what is right and wrong, but I want to focus on our ways of responding when we are faced with an ethical dilemma. In the following section I add my voice to the dialogue.

"We all fail and we all make mistakes"

Sometimes we forget that we are all human and that part of being human is that we make mistakes and fail. It is interesting that it is not simply we who make mistakes but even some great people in the Bible made some bad mistakes. One of them is David. David made several mistakes, but one of the mistakes that the Bible points out is when David slept with Bathsheba, the wife of Uriah. Not only did David sleep with Uriah's wife, but she got pregnant. David tried some tricks to make Uriah sleep with his wife, but Uriah was unwilling to abandon his military responsibilities in the ongoing war. David then used a different plan. He ordered Uriah to fight on the front lines where he was more likely to die. The plan succeeded. Uriah died and David married Uriah's wife Bathsheba (Samuel 2:11). It is worth reflecting on this dimension of the story, not only did David sleep with a married woman but he killed the woman's husband. David committed two major immoral acts and he himself knew that what he did was wrong.

Another example of wrongdoing is found in a story about Peter, who was a close friend to and a disciple of Jesus. After Jesus was arrested, He went to the high priest's house, according to the Gospel of Luke. Peter denied Jesus three times. He denied being with Christ during His ministry's three times (Luke 22:54-62). Peter lied about being with and following Christ.

I selected these two stories to show that we are imperfect, that we all make mistakes and fail. This is part of human nature. The fact that we all make mistakes is not a reason for us to continue failing and not repenting. In the stories of David and Peter we see that they both repented and turned to God and God fulfilled great things through them. Often we humans forget that we all make mistakes and we jump all over someone who has made a mistake as though that person's career is over. Frequently we project an ungodly image on the person who is experiencing a difficult moment. Depending on the reader, it might be difficult to understand my point if you have not failed and had not experienced people trying to take you down. This is very sad and such disrespect can destabilize a person's inner peace.

Motive

A well-known pastor's unmarried daughter got pregnant. Not only was she not married, but the father of the child did not want to marry her. The news reached some churches around the community and the young lady was scorned and excluded from many church-related activities. It is true that many believe that sex outside of marriage is wrong. However, she had already made the mistake and it was not right for Christians in the church to exclude her and reject her. It is right to project, emphasize, preach and teach moral behavior and sanctification. I agree with this, however it is very important to have the right motives. This means that we should be willing to help and uplift people, not put them down or discriminate against them.

If the reader has failed at least once, I want to assure you that the Christian faith is relational. It is not based on what people say but on your relationship with God. Our God sees the positive within the negative. He is not blinded by the negative, but He prioritizes the good He sees. Repent whenever it is needed and know that God forgives.

In this book I have been focusing on finding peace in a broken world and I talk about several occasions in life where we struggle. In this chapter I have focused on those who are oppressed when certain leaders or Christians respond to certain ethical issues at a moment in time. I'm also challenging my readers who may not have been oppressed or victimized to be very careful when dealing with an ethical issue. We must differentiate between good and bad, not accept good for bad but more importantly we must demonstrate Christ and not act hypocritically.

CHAPTER TWELVE

A PEACEFUL AND SUCCESSFUL MINISTRY

Unity   *Humility*   *Service*

Being involved in ministry is very interesting and wonderful. However, it is something that can frustrate you easily or make you feel like quitting. In my limited experience I have listened and read about balancing the ministerial life and personal life. However, in this chapter I'm not dealing with this matter. I am focusing on having a peaceful and successful ministry. At the age of 17 I started to become involved in ministry and since then I have been observing and experiencing both great times in ministry and frustrating moments. There was a period in my life when I personally experienced and observed numerous conflicts at churches. At that time, I asked why people who claim to be Christians couldn't come together and stop fighting over trivial things. This is not only a problem inside of congregations; it is also emerging within doctrinal views. My curiosity motivated me to look for answers. I listened to many sermons about this matter, conducted research and engaged in prayer to find a measure of understanding.

I found out that there are three important concepts that few Christians and Christian leaders understand, practice or prioritize. These three concepts are unity, humility and serving.

These three concepts are important because they highlight what Christians are called to do: live together in love, do ministry in humility and serve as Christ did. In this chapter I will be sharing my points of view and understanding. I interviewed a few people about humility and serving. I could have dedicated an entirely separate chapter or even written a book about each of these concepts had I wished to examine every little detail. However, in this chapter I will try to be specific, deal with the basics and be as brief as possible when discussing unity, humility and serving.

Unity

Unity is very important. In fact, in Jesus' last prayer before His crucifixion, one of the things that Jesus asked the Father was to keep us one, in other words to keep us united (John 17:21-23 NIV). Let me begin by saying that there is no unity without union. In union we bring together different people with different understandings. I was talking with a good friend of mine, whom I call "professor" not because I took a class from him but because I respect his knowledge, his wisdom and his level of critical thinking. I discussed unity with him. He wisely reminded me to recognize that diversity is not division.[19] The meaning of diversity is the

---

[19] Amos Gabriel, Interview by Mardochee Estinvil, San Antonio, June 2017.

state of being diverse and dealing with varieties. Division, on the other hand, is the act of separating something into parts, or the process of being separated. Division often creates breakups, separations and disaffection. When we talk about unity, one of the primary aspects that we need to acknowledge is diversity. I know many people might be frightened by the word diversity. However, it is important to acknowledge that diversity is not a problem and it has never been a problem. The real problem has been our way of managing those differences or our way of living with those differences. Managing or living with differences has created numerous conflicts and divisions in the Christian faith.

I personally share the conviction that diversity was part of God's plan since creation. In fact, in creation or in our universe we find a lot of diversity or contrasts among people and things. One of the enormous differences in creation is what many people have been experiencing on a daily basis— day and night. One day, a 24-hour period, is normally comprised of light during the day and darkness during the night. The list could go on endlessly if we recorded all the diversity in our universe. And examining those differences would simply show that it is the diversity that makes our universe beautiful. This same example is used as a challenge to us in ministry and as human beings. The challenge is to create a beautiful portrait of our differences while we work in unity. In other words, to make a difference while acknowledging our differences from each other as we remain united. In any group of people, whether it is a small or big congregation, the staff or the clergy team need to acknowledge the differences that exist among them and work towards making a difference.

This is a very difficult concept for people to absorb: To make a difference while recognizing our personal differences is challenging. There are three factors that need to be understood: firstly, motive and purpose; secondly, our approach to team work; and thirdly, self-growth. These three qualities have to be both personally and collectively answered. They are equally important because when the motive and purpose are concentrated in glorifying God and fulfilling God's will, one does not see ministry as personal gain. Your love for ministry will move you to care and fight for it, even though you understand it is not yours. For instance, my parents taught me that no church that they ministered was theirs. However, the love that they shared for ministry was remarkably similar to the love that they had for each of their children.

Motive and Purpose

Motive and purpose are essential because they are why you are involved in ministry. In other words, it deals with your objective. It addresses your goals and it speaks about what motivated you to do ministry. When a group's motive and purpose are to fulfill God's ministry and make it a priority, it concentrates on the task at hand and makes it a passion to fulfill that purpose. The focus does not leave room for fighting among themselves. Disagreement in every group is inevitable. However, the resolution will not include putting one another down; the resolution will be framed to allow the goal to be reached in the spirit of love.

It is important for Christian leaders to be motivated with the spirit of love, not one of envy or superiority. It is essential for Christian leaders to understand that we are all part of building the Kingdom of God, therefore we must come together and fulfill God's ministry in unity. The request is not for all doctrines to come together to conform to the exact same principles, however it is to embrace, support and tolerate each difference. In other words, as Stoddard Lane concisely stated, "We agree to differ. We resolve to love. We unite to serve."[20] The intention is not to promote a universal doctrine or a universal church because the diversity that exists within Christianity can be seen in a beautiful way. The idea is to engage even when there are differences, to serve together in those differences and to project love in the midst of those differences. It is better to pursue these goals than fighting among us or asserting one's superiority over the other. The purpose of each Christian ministry should be to focus on God. The motive of each person involved in ministry should be created out of love.

Our Approach to Team Work

The second important feature of unity is the description or the understanding of team work. This involves working as a team or working together. At the very beginning of my discussion on unity, I stated that diversity exists in a group or a team. Now, I'm diving a little deeper to understand how to work together as Christians. It is crucial for Christians to absorb the concept of working together and applying it. I'm convinced that Christianity would face fewer church conflicts and church divisions if Christians could work together.

---

[20] Stoddard Lane (n.d.)

When I was between 14 and 19 years of age, I experienced many church conflicts and church divisions. Even when I came to study in the United State, I observed conflicts among Christians and separations in many Christian groups. And that made me raise the same question that I used to ask: Why are many Christians unable to work in unity?

How many times have we witnessed or examined our work together as a body? How many times have we viewed the congregation as the body of Christ, viewed Christianity as a whole regardless of how many doctrines separate us?

When we view ministry as a body, we pay specific attention to what we are doing to the body. In a body there are many different parts. When one part is damaged, the entire body suffers. Interestingly, all the parts of the body are important and must be doing their job to have a healthy body. For example, the heart is an essential organ in the human body. While the heart is important, if the veins that are connected to the heart are not functioning well, the body is in great danger. So, not only is the heart crucial, but the veins are equally important. In the same way that every single organ is important for the body, every single person is important in the body of Christ. Valuing every single person is essential when it comes to the body of Christ.

Despite the importance of every person, it is harmful for one person to consider himself or herself more important than anyone else. No one is an inevitable asset for the body of Christ to work. Zac Poonen is a minister of several churches in India and has been a bible teacher for over 50 years. He has written more than 25 books.[21] He once gave

---

[21] Zac Poonen," CFC India. http://www.cfcindia.org/zac-poonen.

an important illustration in one of his sermons. He said that if you really want to know how much will be missed in the body of Christ without you do the following. Take a bucket, fill it up with water and put your hands in it and take your hands out. After you take your hands out, see how much water is missing from the bucket. His lesson was not to demonstrate that we are not important in the body, but to show that we should not make too much of ourselves.[22] I strongly believe that humankind and God cooperate in all that God is accomplishing on earth. However, we should not be too prideful of our contributions in His work.

Jesus prayed about unity in His final prayer before his crucifixion: *"My prayer is not for them alone. I pray also for those who will believe in me through their message, that all of them may be one, Father, just as you are in me and I am in you. May they also be in us so that the world may believe that you have sent me"* (John 17:20-21 NIV). To be united, to be as one or to be one is very hard to understand and to apply. A perfect example to illustrate the concept of unity, but which opens space for disagreement, is the Trinity. Due to my awareness of the diversity of understanding and the misunderstanding of many, I won't dive into this example because of the vastness of misunderstandings around the Trinity. However, marriage is a good example that could help us understand the concept of unity. However, because marriage involves only two people, I will use the day of the Pentecost in Acts 2 to illustrate the concept of unity.

The book of Acts in the New Testament skillfully teaches the history of the early church. The book of Acts recounts

---

[22] Zac Poonen, "We Are Not Indispensable," River of Life Christian Fellowship (Twitter blog), October 2017.

many events including the Pentecostal, Peter's miracles, Paul's missionary journeys and many more.[23] Traditionally Luke, one of Jesus' twelve disciples, has been recognized as the author of the Book of Acts. He is also the author of the Gospel of Luke. Some scholarly criticism of Luke state that his work is that of a historian rather than a theologian. They assert that Luke talks more about history in the Gospel of Luke and the Book of Acts rather than projecting his own theology.[24] (Is it true that he is a historian? Let's leave this discussion for the theologians.)

The word Holy Spirit has appeared more than 50 times in the Book of Acts. In the Old Testament we primarily see the picture of the Father as the acting agent; in the Gospels we see the Son Jesus Christ as the acting agent. However, in Acts we see the Holy Spirit as the acting agent.[25] The second chapter of the Book of Acts deals with "The Holy Spirit [coming] upon the apostles and the other believers on the day of the Pentecost"[26] This chapter is one of the favorite chapters of Charismatic Christians when they talk about speaking in tongues or discuss proof of receiving the Holy Spirit. They often declare that speaking in tongues is proof of receiving the Holy Spirit.

---

[23] Joseph Fitzmyer, *Outline of Acts Cornell University, October 2017.* http://www.cornellcollege.edu/classical_studies/greek/outlineofacts.pdf.

[24] David Pawson, *The Normal Christian Birth* (NW1, London: Hodder & Stoughton, 1989), 15.

[25] J. B. Tidwell, *The Bible: Book by Book* (Grand Rapids: Wm. B. Berdmans, 1950).

[26] Steven J. Cole, "Lesson 4: The Meaning of Pentecost." Bible. org. August 6, 2013. https://bible.org/seriespage/lesson-4-meaning-pentecost-acts-21-13

I refer to Acts 2 not to discuss the Holy Spirit. I refer to Acts 2 to demonstrate that the Holy Spirit came on the day of the Pentecost when Peter preached a powerful sermon that resulted in the conversion of numerous people. *"All the believers were together and had everything in common."* (Acts 2: 44 NIV). Scripture also tells us in Acts 2, *"They sold property and possessions to give to anyone who had need. Every day they continued to meet together in the temple courts. They broke bread in their homes and ate together with glad and sincere hearts, praising God and enjoying the favor of all the people. And the Lord added to their number daily those who were being saved."* (Acts 2:45-47 NIV). Please note that the Holy Spirit unified and the Holy Spirit brought these people together and unified them to a level of sincerely caring for each other. Where one was willing to sacrifice his or her own belongings to give to one in need is clearly a sign of feeling kinship. This is a perfect example of working and living together toward a common goal.

Today I'm not requesting that deep level of sacrifice, I'm simply longing for the willingness to understand and work as a team. It is essential for us to understand that we are all part of the same body. When one organ or member is affected, the whole body is also affected. It is important to see the team as one. Our differences should not prevent us from making a difference when we are working together.

Self-growth

This third feature is how to deal with conflict. It is sad to say but conflicts, misunderstandings and other problems are inevitable when people work or live together. These are simply challenges in creating unity and they should not stop us from working together. We must adopt a mindset to face these challenges in the correct way. At the beginning of this chapter I mentioned that I had observed many church conflicts and fighting among Christians which moved me to raise some questions. Conflicts, misunderstandings and other forms of disagreement are inevitable; however, these things shouldn't create separation among us. These moments of conflict should have provided an opportunity for the group to become stronger and more unified. However, since a group is comprised of separate parts, each part must be healthy to create a healthier whole. The self-growth feature focuses on three areas: maturity, selfishness or self-centeredness and the need for the love of tolerance.

Maturity

There are different stages of maturity just as there are different types of maturity. Maturity refers to a person who is responsible for themselves. Emotional maturity means that someone is stable and well adjusted. Even if a person is physically independent and responsible for themselves, they may be emotionally unstable. Such people might own a big house, have three or four cars and be financially sound, but their emotional life is as undeveloped as a baby's. Maturity is often defined by one's age group or one's physical appearance. From this point of view the person can appear to be mature, however I have observed numerous times that there are fourteen-year-olds who are more mature than many 21-year old. Embedded inside of the word maturity we find the word mature, which can be understood as full-grown or independent. In other words, the word mature can mean that a person is not dependent on others. In this chapter, I use maturity as a quality that Christians need to learn. It is an indispensable quality needed among members of a group to build cooperation and to work as a team.

Our actions and reactions are two behaviors that show others about our level of maturity. When we act or react in a mature way, it sends a clear message and makes space for tolerance. What is the character of a mature person?

For Professor Amos Gabriel, maturity is revealed in the ways we act and react. For Gabriel, a mature person will react to a moment of conflict with wisdom and love. For him, moments of conflict and misunderstanding are moments when love should triumph rather than the ambition to put one down. When we act and react in a spiritually mature way, we reflect God. However, Professor Gabriel does not think that we can reach that level with our own intelligence; he believes that we need the Holy Spirit to move in us.[27]

Selfish or Self-centeredness

We are all, in some measure, selfish or self-centered. It is our instinct to look out for ourselves first. However, when we are working in unity it is very important to look out for the team, not to look out for ourselves. In unity we do not come first. Selfishness can block group success. It can impede reaching an agreement, establishing goals or engaging in strategies to achieve a goal. For a team to be effective and successful, it is essential to put aside one's

---

[27] Amos Gabriel, Interview by Mardochee Estinvil, San Antonio, October 23, 2017.

self-interest. It is not about who is the smartest or who is the most vocal. To fully love and to fully care we must let our egos rest. We must be willing to sacrifice for the greater good.

Tolerance

The final feature of unity is the love of tolerance. It is good for a leader to be strict, but it is also important for a leader not to have a legalistic approach to taking charge. When working together toward a common goal there is no right or wrong or black or white. The approach must be more nuanced and diplomatic. Humans always make mistakes; no human other than Jesus Christ is perfect. Imperfection is part of human nature. (This is not an invitation to keep on making mistakes). This reminds us that it is important to embrace certain failures and misunderstandings with other members of the team. The love of tolerance does not mean we do not fight for change or challenge others. However, it is to love in patience, love in kindness and love in forgiveness. When we apply these attributes, the chance for improvement becomes possible and the team will grow with a stronger spirit of unity.

Humility

Humility is a difficult concept to define. It is visible through the act of service and through our behavior during difficult times. The proof of humility through the act of service does not mean that serving equals humility. When we serve in humility it is revealed to others. Humility is easily misunderstood. It is important to be clear that *humility is not equal to silence.* That does not mean that a humble person won't be silent at times but being quiet does not mean being humble. You can be a very talkative person and be a very humble person. Humility does not mean acceptance of everything either.

There is not an accurate measurement for humility. Deep inside of us we all carry a level of humility. How much humility do we need?

When I asked Professor Amos Gabriel about humility, he pointed out that humility is a choice, it is a voluntary decision. And in contrast humiliation is often not a choice, it is one that we do not get to choose and we do not like.[28] However, humiliation is one that Jesus faced in His ministry and is also one that we face numerous times in ministry.

In the description of the first point, Professor Gabriel mentioned that every single person is born with at least two gifts from the Lord. These two gifts are dignity and freedom. The word dignity is originated from Latin which is dingus. Based on oxforddictionaries.com the word dignity means "The state or quality of being worthy of honor or respect."[29] Professor Gabriel believes that every person is born in the image of God, and that they are also born with dignity. However, he cautioned that dignity is something that needs to be balanced. If we have a low understanding of our dignity, then we have low self-esteem. And if we have too high an opinion of our own dignity, we are likely to create an inflated self-ego. According to Professor Gabriel,

---

[28] Amos Gabriel, Phone Interview by Mardochee Estinvil, San Antonio, October 2017.
[29] Oxforddictionaries.com. https://en.oxforddictionaries.com/definition/dignity.

when we talk about embracing humiliation it does not mean to lose your dignity or self. In contrast, it is to willingly choose to embrace humiliation without diminishing who you are.

When we look at the life of Jesus, how He willingly embraced humiliation and endured the cross for us, we can honestly agree with Professor Gabriel on embracing humiliation without diminishing who we are. Jesus, the Son of God, left His throne and incarnated as a human being. He not only died on the cross for our sins, but he also brought light to humanity by revealing His Heavenly Father's love. And He did so, throughout His life. For Jesus to fulfill His calling on earth, He willingly embraced humiliation for us.

Although Jesus willingly embraced humiliation that did not make Him less than what He was, in other words He never lost His dignity. In fact, these actions of humility and embracement of humiliations exalted Him in such measure, where the Father *"gave Him the name that is above every name, that at the name of Jesus every knee should bow, in heaven and on earth and under the earth, and every tongue acknowledge that Jesus Christ is Lord, to the glory of God, the Father."* (Philippians 2:9b-11). Today, the type of humility that needs to be practiced in ministry is one of willingness to embrace humiliation. Not that we lose our dignity, however, we willingly embrace it, as our own cross.

In the ministry of Jesus, there are two biblical portions about Him embracing humiliation that shake my entire being. The first one is when the crowd chose Barabbas to be released over Jesus. (Matthew 27:15-21 NIV). The second one is when *"Jesus' cried out in a loud voice, "Eli, Eli, lema sabachthani?" ("My God, my God, why have you forsaken me?")"* (Matthew 27:46 NIV).

In spite of all the difficulties that Jesus faced in His ministry, including the 40 days of fasting, the temptations after the 40 days of fasting, from the four biblical accounts that we have on Jesus' life it has been mentioned only at one point in His life where Jesus asked His Father why have you forsaken me? And that one time in Jesus' life was when He was on the cross carrying our sins. At that moment the Father had forsaken Him. The Father did so not because He did not love Him, but simply because of the sinful nature that Jesus was in. Jesus was in that sinful nature simply because He was carrying the sins of humanity. He embraced humiliation and shame, in humility. He did so for the greater good of humanity, where today many of us can say that we are children of God or that the relationship between child and parent is being rebuilt between us and God.

Today I'm not sending anyone to a place or a position where God has to forsake you. This was and had to be done once. If this happens to you, know there is something wrong in the relationship with God. My point is to project what Jesus Christ, the one who we are following, has gone through and to consider that anything that we might face in ministry and in life is much less than what Jesus faced. In other words, we need to be willing to embrace in humility certain things that we will face on our journey walking with God. Many times, when we face difficulties in ministries, we tend to be troubled or show our ego, while it is the best place for humility to reveal itself within us.

Humility is essential in ministry. If we can dive into the deepest level of humility, which is the willingness to embrace humiliation, then I'm sure that the practice of humility toward one another will be much easier to accept.

Service

There is a distinct difference between someone who serves and a true servant. Anyone can serve, but not all of those who serve are really serving with a sincere motive or with the right attitude. It is not my job to judge whether or not someone has the right motive, however, it is important to understand what service is and to understand the type of servants that Christ looks for. The importance of caring, kindness and love in service are indispensable as are the adoption of strategies to serve successfully and consistently.

Service can be defined has "an act of helpful activity or to supply utilities or commendation"[30] that people need. In other words, it is to offer a service that people need. It is important to remember that we are all called to serve at some level. Also, Christians are not simply called to serve, but the Christian way of serving is equally important in ministry. Jesus did not simply serve others, but He lived a servant's life. He lived a life where He fulfilled His Father's will and completely obeyed His Father's will throughout His life. The concept of service is very important in ministry and many times Christians and even Christian leaders do not pay attention to why they are serving and what would make them a good servant. What is the difference? What do these two mean?

To serve in the ministry is not to serve for personal gain or for public recognition, but serving others is a way of

---

[30] http://www.dictionary.com/browse/service

living in which the person demonstrates Christ. The person serving is helping to build the Kingdom of God. In other words, the work of a servant in ministry is to help build and reveal the Kingdom of God. Sadly, when I was a teenager, I saw leaders serving in worship ministry, teaching ministry and other ministries inside the church, dividing the church that they were serving in. At other times they were not dividing the church, but they were exhibiting a conflict of interest that damaged the wellbeing of the church. I strongly believe that if they had had a better understanding of service and serving others, their behavior would have been much different.

I interviewed Dr. Sandee Gray Elizondo, one of my undergraduate leadership professors, for this section on service. She has experience teaching and serving in ministry. (She has a passionate heart for teaching). Here I present a few of the features of service we discussed. Dr. Elizondo explained how her understanding of service changed from before and after she studied it. Initially, her understanding of service was simply that it was an obligation or an act that we have to do. However, after she studied it, she came to understand service has a discipline. The practice of service brings transformation to our lives and it is something that needs to be done in humility, in hiddenness and with love. One of her powerful messages was that we serve to uplift people. She also mentioned the names of some scholars who influenced her understanding of service: Robert K. Greenleaf's body of writing, Richard J. Foster's *Celebration of Discipline* and Leighton Ford's *Transforming Leadership*.

Dr. Elizondo also addressed the dangers in serving

which is to serve only those who we love and serving to show off to others. Let me elaborate on a few of her ideas.[31]

Serving is very important and we are not simply called to do the act of serving in the Christian faith, we are called to be servants. Humility is very important and one passage of scripture that Dr. Elizondo referred to is when "Jesus washed the disciples' feet." (John 13:1-17 NIV). Jesus humbled Himself regardless of who He was and willingly washed the disciples' feet. Two interesting things about the passage is Peter's first comment to Jesus and the act of washing the disciples' feet. It would have been culturally appropriate for the disciples to wash Jesus' feet but not Jesus washing their feet. In that ancient world, slaves were looked down on and it was very difficult for Peter to accept Jesus washing his feet because it mirrored the act of a slave.[32] Secondly, people walked everywhere, so the disciples' feet were dusty and dirty, yet Jesus humbled Himself to clean their feet.

Serving in hiddenness keeps our service invisible because we do not serve to show others that we are serving. Even though our acts of service can impact someone's life, our anonymity keeps our service private. It is very important not to do an act of service to gain attention. (I have seen many people in ministry who do an act of service just to gain attention).

Serving in love is very important. It challenges our purpose in serving and it demonstrates how far the servant is

---

[31] Sandee Gray Elizondo, Interview by Mardochee Estinvil, San Antonio, April 25, 2018.

[32] Bible Gateway.com, accessed June 01, 2018. https://www.biblegateway.com/resources/commentaries/IVP-NT/John/Jesus-Washes-Disciples-Feet.

willing to go. Jesus served in love and demonstrated love in all of His acts of service. Jesus' love and passion for serving others was so strong that He found purpose in serving till the very end of His life. When we serve in love we experience transformation in it and we transform more to the likeness of Christ.

Dangers

It is easy to serve those we like and love, but the act of service is one that needs to be shared with everyone regardless of their gender, ethnicity and beliefs. Dr. Elizondo said that "we are all made in the image of God. It makes me no different from another person." She used another powerful phrase that is important to reflect on: "It is important to remember that I'm a great sinner and how can I treat others less?"[33] It is very easy to be tempted to serve certain groups and not others, but it is dangerous to do so. A servant needs to be filled with an unconditional loving spirit, a spirit to serve everyone regardless of who they are. Jesus paid great attention and served those who were most in need. Serving is not to show others we served, but it is an act to uplift and help others.

To conclude this section of service, it is important to look at the perfect example of a good servant—any loving mother. It is fascinating to see how a mother lovingly serves her children. Though her child will undoubtedly create problems, a mother will not stop loving and caring and serving her child. A loving mother gives her best to her

---

[33] Sandee Gray Elizondo, Interview by Mardochee Estinvil, April 25, 2018.

children and will not allow small matters to discourage her from serving her children. In the same way, we need Christian leaders in ministry to embrace the spirit of a loving mother. Leaders who serve in love will not allow certain problems to divide their ministry. The inability to understand what service is and why we serve can create dissent and division to a ministry.

CHAPTER THIRTEEN

OUR CONTRIBUTION AND SUPPORT

I want to admit that when I started to write this book, I observed things on a personal level. I believed that for someone to be at peace it only takes a personal commitment to achieve it. A personal dimension is needed to achieve internal peace, but it can also require the contributions of others to find peace. The contributions and support of others can help us to more easily overcome certain obstacles. I realized this when I started to interview several people and gained a deep understanding of their experiences. While conducting research I found out that everyone who had a group of friends or family members and some church members available to support them during their emotionally challenging times, were able to overcome the challenging moment faster. For example, when many were suffering depression their supportive network reached out and helped them to recover more quickly. Sadly, those who did not have such support experienced a difficult and lonely journey.

One of the people I interviewed had suffered depression for eleven years. He experienced highs and lows. Some days, he would feel normal and other days he felt lost and broken.

Several times he attempted suicide and involved himself in activities in an effort to feel better. He drank, smoked and became sexually active with numerous women. He had spoken about his depression with his church leaders many times, but sadly their advice was to pray more and not pursue professional medical treatment. I strongly believe in prayer, however sometimes it is not the correct advice to encourage only prayer when there is a serious psychological and emotional problem. In this case, it was not enough to tell the troubled person to keep praying and that you will keep him in your prayers. It is not acting responsibly when the person needs to speak to a medical expert or someone who can give him or her professional assistance.

It is a tragedy that numerous people are committing suicide daily. The number of people living with depression, fear and insecurity nowadays is staggering. It is equally sad that members of our churches are also suffering and they are not receiving sufficient support. My intention is not to blame the church or anyone else, it is to bring awareness to the forefront and offer some possible solutions. I do not think that we can completely eliminate these problems nor cure everyone. I wish that we could. However, we can have a role in the fight against this epidemic. In other words, we can help others overcome depression, fear and insecurity.

The first two weeks after I arrived in the United States in 2014 for my studies, I found myself feeling alone. Every time I went to a grocery store or some other busy place, I would greet people like I had done in Haiti. However, I quickly realized that almost no one responded. I noticed that people in the U.S. were private and not accustomed to speaking to strangers. The culture promoted individualism and everyone was out for themselves. This type of society can be good sometimes, but it was totally foreign to me when I arrived. Since then I have built the mentality that everyone is doing just fine. After about two years I realized that many of the people I knew were actually experiencing some hardship. If I had opened myself up to them I could have possibly helped them in some way. There are two ideas I want to impart from this story. Firstly, in individualistic places there is still the need for a community. Secondly, someone might look alright, but it does not mean that they are. They might be struggling with a problem that you could help them to resolve.

In my understanding there are at least two ways that we can contribute and offer support to others. We can create a safe environment where others can be open and honest. And we can be more sensitive to the problems around us. I will elaborate on these two concepts here.

Creating an Atmosphere

Creating a safe atmosphere where friends, family and others can be open about their life and struggles is very important. We are called to live in a community and to have fellowship with one another as a way to connect. We cannot live alone; we all need other people in some measure. This is not a reason to be dependent on others for everything. However, it is to understand that we usually find ourselves within the circle of relationships or community and in these types of circles there is the urgency to create a healthy atmosphere where we can share our feelings with each other. There are different types of relationship circles, but in this section I'll address three fundamental areas or circles where there is the need to establish a good atmosphere. These three circles are at a personal or one on one level, within the family and at church.

One on One

The personal level challenges our willingness to create an atmosphere where your close friends or the ones who are closest to you can feel safe enough to share their own issues with you. In this circle there is the need to establish trust and to exhibit an openness that will demonstrate to the other person that you are there for him or her. Being a close friend is not being someone that only enjoys the good times, but it is someone who is ready to support the other person during the difficult times as well. It is someone that is available to give you advice when life is shaky. It is someone who can talk to you when you are heading in the wrong direction. Be a friend who can listen, understand and offer support.

Family Circle

The circle of family is often considered the most important and the most fragile circle. The atmosphere at home with family members influences our character, our lifestyle and our ability to navigate life's challenges. One of the interesting things I discovered in my research was that many variables that cause depression and other related problems are connected to our families. Family separations or behaviors within or outside the house related to family members can negatively impact someone's life. Family is very important and we cannot create a healthy society without promoting improvements within our families. What happens at home certainly impacts society at large. Therefore, it is important to focus on a healthy family atmosphere.

A family is composed of parents and kids, and both of these entities are equally important. It is important for the kids or the children to see a parent as a friend with whom they can share their feelings and experiences. A parent plays different roles in the lives of their children. They can be a friend but they must also show their children that they support them and understand them. It is important to establish a trusting relationship. The atmosphere within the family circle is not just important for the children, it's also important for the parents. As a spouse, it is important to be supportive of your partner, to be available to talk about important matters and to share feelings.

When there is that level of trust and openness within the family a healthy environment is created. When one is going through a problem neither the children nor the parents will be afraid to bring it to the circle because he or she knows the family is there for support and help. A healthy family atmosphere helps in at least two different ways. Firstly, helps one understand that they do not need to carry the problem alone and that support is available from a loved one. Secondly, it shows children that the best way to overcome difficulty is not through drug use or behaving badly, but from talking about their problems with loved ones and by taking a positive initiative.

The Church Circle

The church circle is a very important circle, although it does not hold the same importance as the family circle. The church circle should influence the other two circles. When I refer to the church, I'm not talking about a church building or place where people come together to pray and worship. When I mention church I'm referring to a large family of faith. I'm referring to a spiritual congregation that is one in Christ. I'm referring to the body of Christ. Both worshiping and praying play an essential role within the church circle, but these two features are not the only things that fully describe the church.

The church is a large family of faith; we refer to each other as brothers and sisters in Christ. However, it is important to question the atmosphere within the church. Do we really live as brothers and sisters? Or is it just a saying? I'm not criticizing all churches; in fact, some churches do their very best in working through difficulties with members of their congregation. When close family members of mine lost their son a few weeks after the summer of 2017, they found support at their church. Their son was a good man with great potential who was studying at college. Unexpectedly the family received the news that their son had passed away. It was and still is a tough journey for this family. When the family talks about how they are walking through this difficult time, they feel blessed by the support of their local church. Their church stands with them and walks through this journey with them. My point is not to criticize the church, but it is to help us think or re-think the importance of the church's contribution and how it supports its members.

The church is far more than worshiping and praying together. It has the mission to engage in each member's life journey. When sister H has a problem, it's not only her problem. It becomes a problem her large family of faith also takes on and helps her to work through. When brother P has a problem, it's not his to handle alone. He has the large family of faith to walk through the difficult moments with him. For this to happen we shouldn't embrace the concept of sola handle (you handle it alone), but instead we should create an atmosphere within the church that is all inclusive. It needs to be one of a loving family and a loving community.

For a church to be supportive of its members, there are at least three areas that we need to consider: teaching and preaching, small groups and activities that bring people together. The sermons and other forms of teaching play a very important role in the church, but sometimes this activity can be monopolized by one topic and does not leave space for the discussion of other subjects. For example, numerous churches focus on sermons about miracles and physical blessings and leave little time to preach about family, depression or fear and anxiety.

Small groups are very important because they provide members with a place to engage in conversations about life. For example, if brother P is going through some difficulties, he can share his experiences with the small group. In turn the group can support him through prayer, advice or shared experiences. The small group can give some other form of assistance to brother P. Often we underestimate the power of sharing. It is good for people to have a place where they can talk about life. When people see that a group listens to them, that a group prays with them and are there for them, they begin to understand that they are not alone and that others are living in a loneliness circle as well.

Remarkably, churches can grow as they engage in activities that bring people together. In 2012 my home church in Bois Pernier, Port-au-Prince, Haiti was building a cafeteria. There were materials to build it, but the church members had to rally and construct it themselves. The congregants were the first to do so, and once they did, people from the greater community came and joined the work effort. The church members and the people from the community worked in different capacities. For example, a group of women cooked, and construction guys did their part, while others transported water and other materials. This activity had helped to increase the size of the church, the number of people attending the church and most significantly it had helped improve the harmony among the people in the church. What I mean by this is that it had helped everyone to get to know each other better, which helped to increase the spirit of a larger family of faith inside of the church.

Over the past few years I have been working with different missionary teams and at times I have taken some mission trips to Haiti. I have observed that churches that become involved in such activities tend to grow in size and nurture the strengthening spirit of a larger family. It is because they have experienced a journey together that they feel a sense of kinship with each other. Many youths had that experience when they discovered their calling or improved their relationship with God. I found my calling to ministry during a similar experience. I started my spiritual growth and found the desire to serve the Lord with all my heart when I was involved in church activities.

From my own personal experience, I believe it is when we step into God's work and start involving ourselves that we find solutions to our problems. It is a mysterious sensation that I cannot really explain, but when we step into God's work we no longer focus on "I" but rather on God's will. And it is during these moments that we often find the solutions, the answers to our problems or we find tranquility in our problem. I am not instructing churches to become involved in construction to engage members since it might not work the same way in every church. It is not to tell all churches to do mission trips to Haiti, because not all churches might be called to Haiti. However, it is to challenge to churches to take the initiative and create activities that can bring people together. These activities will help improve the family atmosphere in the church and help many congregants find solutions to their problems.

My mom often told her children, "Don't simply tell me that you love me but show me that you love me. When I look at the commandments of Christ in loving one another I do not think that he was saying to just tell your brother or sister that you love them. It is also to demonstrate that love to your brother and sister through your behaviors and the support that you give them. Be supportive and join them in their journey in life. We have to create a safe and loving atmosphere, an atmosphere where our brothers, sisters and others can be open and honest."

Being Aware

In the first circle we created a welcoming and safe atmosphere. Now we are going to move a little bit forward. Frequently we cannot see peoples' pain in their faces. Their faces do not reveal what their problems might be. The church is a large family of faith and we are part of this large family of faith, so it is important for us to be aware or use strategies to identify if a problem is present. Not only will our sensitivity help us to sense a problem, but it will also help us understand the problem. The better we understand the problems and their causes the more valuable we will be in finding a solution.

It takes little effort to notice that there is a problem. We can start by asking some simple questions. If you are a church leader you can ask some of the following questions. How many married couple do we have in the church? How many single moms do we have in the church? How many youths do we have? How old are the youth? How many children are there? What's their story? Once you begin to ask questions you demonstrate curiosity and you can explore Further questioning can bring answers. What are the problems that each of these groups face? How can we help and walk this journey with them?

Nowadays we hear the repetitive sermon of material blessings. It has been preached over and over again. I'm not against this type of sermon, but sometimes I wish we could have some seminars or group meetings where couples can come and talk about their marriages. Sometimes, I wish we could help or be more supportive to single moms, because their journey is difficult, and we have a large family of faith to give support. The problem of sister H must concern the church. However, we cannot be supportive to different groups if there is no awareness or sensitivity. Once there is greater awareness of people's problems we can become engaged and offer our contributions and support.

I apologize to anybody if by accident this chapter offended you. As I already mentioned, my point is to help us think or re-think our contributions and support. I, too, am guilty of falling short in many of these areas. When I say church do not simply think of your pastor or the leader at your church. You are also included. It's *our* contribution. We are the church. We are part of the larger family of faith. Let us not blame one person or a group of leaders but let us all be challenged and held responsible.

CONCLUSION

There are more themes and stories I wish I could cover in this book. However, this is why this is volume one and in volume two I will move forward to discuss other topics. While I'm very excited for the second volume, I hope the information in this book can help my readers to live a more peaceful life by helping them to develop a different mindset.

In this book I have not focused on deliverance and miracles since these themes are often preached about in sermons. Neither have I focused on the second coming of Jesus. It is not because I ignore the importance of that event or value it less than others do. In fact, I cannot wait for my Savior's return. However, it is because life is a journey, a journey that the believers in Christ do not walk alone. On the contrary, they walk together with Christ. Therefore, I can walk peacefully even though the current reality or moment might be very difficult. It is similar to our experiences as a child—we have a daddy. He is a daddy who loves and cares for us more than we can care for our own selves. A daddy who sent His most precious one Jesus to come die on the cross for us, and through the crucifixion of Jesus we can build a relationship with the God of the universe.

Dear friends, I'm begging you to remain and abide

in Christ. Salvation, peace and love are not in us, but all of these precious things are in Christ. Therefore, keep on believing and abiding in whom all power was given. Our own Savior Jesus Christ.

Dear friends, be wise in all situations that involve caution and patience. Be careful in your interpretation and how we communicate with God. It is very important to be honest with God. This is not a license to doubt or question His authority. Timing is His and it is very difficult for us to understand His work unless we are patient.

May the God of the universe
Enrich you with all the fruits of the Spirit
And to guide you along the way

MEET THE AUTHOR

I'm the second child of my parents. My father is the senior minister of Mission Calvaire Baptist de la redemption in Haiti. In this mission there are over sixteen churches. My mother is the founder of First Fruit Haiti. First Fruit is a non-profit organization located in Port-au-Prince which provides services in different cities throughout the country. In 1985, this ministry started by building home gardens for people who were in need. The purpose of this organization is to reach out beyond the walls of the church with the love of Christ.

One of the most inspiring and impactful faith-based stories I have heard in my life is the testimony of my grandmother, my mother's mother. She was born in a non-Christian family. When my grandmother wanted to become a Christian, she abandoned her entire family and sacrificed all her possessions to follow Christ. In her conversion she burned even the dress that she was wearing. She started from zero. When my mother was five years old and my aunt Valine was six months, my grandmother's husband died. She decided to remain a single mom until her daughters would be able to take care of themselves. She fought with life regardless of how poor she was at that time. Although she did not have a comfortable place to live, her belief in God and in the importance of education moved her to pass these values onto her daughters.

One of the core values in her faithful life was the fear of the Lord. She believed in God as a loving father, but she also believed that if we want to follow Jesus we must pay attention to our actions and reactions. She saw God as her ultimate option in life. So, in her life she experienced God as a provider, a healer, a father and a friend through Jesus Christ.

In the last seventeen years of her life she battled cancer. In her last week she was hospitalized. While I was worried about her leaving us, she was singing the song *The King of Love My Shepherd Is*.

> *The King of love my shepherd is,*
> *Whose goodness faileth never,*
> *I nothing lack if I am his*
> *And he is mine forever.*

Even through all that she had gone in life her final words were words of gratitude and praise to God. At her funeral, more than eight people came to Christ and these were people who had lived close to her and had observed her life. And through their observations of her life, her life influenced them to Christ. There is not a record of how many people she had brought to Christ during her lifetime or how many people have come to Christ after she died. However, I have heard countless testimonies of people acknowledging my grandmother, talking about how she impacted their lives and how her style of living influenced them to become a disciple of Jesus.

One interesting story I have heard from people who knew her for close to ten years was how she would attract them with a generous cup of coffee and bread and sit and talk to them. It was in that same neighborhood where I first became involved in ministry. She was an excellent listener and a wise adviser who was a revered mother figure for many in this community.

The main things in her life that influenced me were her perseverance in faith and her acceptance of the present, since faith guaranties a great future even if our understanding of a great future is different from God's grand plan. She was a servant who was willing to do anything. In fact, one of her ministries was cleaning the church, a ministry that is rarely acknowledged by congregants or pastors. My grandmother's name was Valissia Valmon Telemaque and I proudly declare that I was very close to her. (Although, my older brother was her favorite).

I have to admit that even all of these influences in my background did not move me to commit to ministry full time. I didn't want to be in ministry full time or as dedicated as my parents were. The only thing I wanted to do in ministry was preaching. (Maybe it was because at a young age I had observed the sacrifice my parents made for ministry.) I wanted to be a preacher and be a guest speaker, but I did not want to be involved full time in any church simply to avoid problems in ministry. Little by little my perceptions changed and I decided that I would become involved in ministry when I'm in my late 40s or early 50s. However, when I was fourteen years old God showed me something different and He called me. After the earthquake on January 12, 2010 I understood that the biggest thing in life is to help and serve others. It's not about what you possess because at the blink of an eye everything can be gone. That is not to discourage anyone from having some nice things, but don't live for accumulating possessions. Regardless of my position in life, to serve and help others should be my goal. I was the last person in my family to make the decision to become a Christian. It happened when I was thirteen years old, in October 2008. Four years later I was baptized.

One of the most significant periods of my life was from January 2010 to August 2014. This is when I discovered who I really am and found my purpose in life. In these four years I experienced so many unbelievable things in ministry, both in a positive way and a negative way as I struggled with some difficulties. I faced situations that brought more trust and hope in my life, but also things that made me think deeply and raised some deep theological questions. I thank God for those theological questions, because it has helped me to pursue a deeper understanding of Him.

One the most miraculous moments in my life was when I was fretting about going to college in 2011 and 2012. In the fall of 2012, I had the privilege to work with a mission team from the U.S. Over several days the team had visited a lot of my parents' ministries and at the end of this tour the senior pastor of the church team declared, "I have seen all these projects, but the main priority we would like to focus on is to send this boy to college." That was a powerful statement for me and my family. Our focus had been just that, but we had never mentioned it to anyone on the team.

I have to say that after the minister said that I started to understand that God loves me more than I personally love myself. And if He loves me that much, He also cares for me that much. Therefore, my only job is to trust and obey Him. When the minister spoke about going to college it made me realize that I had a greater purpose. And this was enough for me. When I heard the minister's words, I no longer cared about going to college. I saw that God cares about others and this taught me at that moment about the profound care God had for my life. This was a miraculous moment for me during those four years.

I want to point out two more things about myself. The first one is that at a very young age I had the opportunity to observe doctrinal differences. My dad is a Baptist minister, my grandmother was a Pentecostal, and I identify my mom as a mixture of both Baptist and Pentecostal. A lot of my high school professors were Jehovah Witnesses. A good number of my friends were Seventh Day Adventists and many of my friends were Catholic. (There are many more Christian doctrines that could be listed here.) In each of these doctrines I have met great people who have great hearts, people with great love to share for the Lord and people with high levels of moral discipline. This brought me to a place where I don't prioritize one doctrine over the other. I respect each doctrine and each person who follows a different doctrine. However, no doctrine is perfect and there is at least one positive lesson for us to learn from each Christian doctrine. So, I'm not a guy who really belongs to a single denomination nor do I prioritize one over the other.

From 2010 to 2014 I had shifted somewhat in my interest in ministry. At the very beginning my interest was all about bringing people to Christ, but my focus now is not that. My focus is mainly on the area of discipleship, improving the quality of the life we live as Christians. It is true that to be a Christian there is a day to start, the day when someone chooses to give his/her life to Christ. However, this process is only the beginning. It's the beginning of a new relationship; it's a walk with Christ. I'm not interested in a one-day decision, but a decision that starts one day with the goal to remain and abide in Christ. I'm very grateful to the Lord for inspiring me to write this book, which is mainly addressed to born-again Christians and challenges a non-Christian to lead a faithful life of pursuing and abiding in Christ.

BIBLIOGRAPHY

Boom, Corrie Ten. *Clippings from my notebook: writings and sayings collected*. Minneapolis: Worldwide Publications, 1984.

Cole, Steven J. *"Lesson 4: The Meaning of Pentecost,"* Bible. org. August 6, 2013. https://bible.org/seriespage/lesson-4-meaning-pentecost-acts-21-13

Dictionary.com. *"Self-control,"* accessed October 11, 2018. https://www.dictionary.com/browse/self-control.

Dictionary.com. *"Service,"* accessed April 23, 2018. http://www.dictionary.com/browse/service

Fitzmyer, Joseph. *"Outline of Acts Cornell University,"* http://www.cornellcollege.edu/classical_studies/greek/outlineofacts.pdf.

Hastings, James ed. *"The Great Texts of the Bible, Vol. 3."* Grand Rapids, Michigan: Wm. B. Eerdmans, 1958.

Hendriksen, William. *New Testament Commentary on Matthew*. Grand Rapids: Baker Pub Group, 1978.

Hymn Alnet RSS. *"What a Friend we have in Jesus."* Accessed January 3, 2018. https://www.hymnal.net/en/home

JW.ORG. "Learn From Me." Accessed February 3, 2019. https://wol.jw.org/en/wol/d/r1/lp- e/2001923.

"Jesus Washes His Disciples' Feet." Accessed June 01, 2018.
https://www.biblegateway.com/resources/commentaries
/IVP-NT/John/Jesus-Washes-Disciples-Feet.

Morgan, G. Campbell. *The Gospel According to John*, 317.
London and Edinburgh: Fleming H. Revell Company.

Morgan, Robert J. *Then Sings My Soul*. Nashville: Thomas
Nelson Publisher, 2003.

Oxforddictionaries.com. https://en.oxforddictionaries.com/
definition/dignity.

Pawson, David. *The Normal Christian Birth*. London: NW1,
Hodder & Stoughton, 1989.

Poonen, Zac. CFC India. http://www.cfcindia.org/zac-
poonen.

Poonen, Zac. *"We Are Not Indispensable."* Twitter blog, n.d.
River of Life Christian Fellowship.

Raising godly children. *"16 House Rules by Susannah Wesley
(John Wesley's Mom)."* May 08, 2016. Accessed May 26,
2018. http://www.raisinggodlychildren.org/2011/03/16-
house-rules-by-susannah-wesley-john-wesleys-mom.
html.

Robertson, Archibald Thomas. *Word Pictures in the New
Testament John and Hebrews vol. V*. Nashville: Broad
Man Press, 1932.

Stuarts Draft Retirement Community (blog*). "The Story
Behind the Hymn: What a Friend We Have in Jesus."*
October 30, 2013. Accessed January 03, 2018.
http://www.sdretire.com

Stoddard Lane (n.d.)

The Interpreter's Bible, Vol. 7: *"New Testament Articles
Matthew and Mark."* New York: Abingdon Press
Nashville.

Tidwell, J. B. "*The Bible: Book by Book.*" Grand Rapids: Wm. B. Berdmans, 1950.

United Methodist Videos. "*Susanna Wesley: Mother of Methodism.*" YouTube: April 07, 2016.
Accessed May 26, 2018. https://www.youtube.com/watch?v=Zpi1OJ5LiVY.

Bible Version: ESV, NIV, KJV, NRSV.

Printed in the United States
By Bookmasters